The Icing on Top Ain't Always Sweet

A Novel By

MZ. SKITTLEZ

This book is a work of fiction. The characters, incidents, and dialogue are drawn from the author's imagination and are not to be construed as real. Any resemblance to actual events or persons, living or dead, is entirely coincidental.

Books may be purchase for educational, business, or sale promotional use. For information, please contact the author using the contact information provided at the end of the book.

First Edition

Copyright © 2014

Note from the Author

This book is for people that thought about giving up, and people that think their ideas are too big to fulfill. People who think they need investors to grow their business from the start. All moguls started with a dollar and a dream. Never give up or take no for an answer! It's yours if you want it bad enough... you can turn every tragedy to triumph.

1

"Without pressure, there would be no diamonds. It's how you cope with life's difficult situations that determine how you shine..."

It was a cold, stormy evening, the night my life changed forever. Freezing rain pelted against the windshield of the Penske moving truck and my mother's knuckles turned white as she gripped the steering wheel tightly. Playing softly on the radio was the Commodore's classic "*Zoom*." In the back seat, I sat wide-eyed. My brother, Avon sat on one side of me while our eldest brother, James sat on the other. As my mother fled our hometown, I felt afraid and confused as to why I was suddenly being uprooted from my life in Cleveland. Diane was taking everything away from me that I loved and cherished in Ohio, including my father. Upon asking, my mother simply stated that it was "God's will." That was her answer for everything. For as long as I could remember, my mother had always used the Lord to justify any and every situation, even the less than logical ones like driving to another state to pursue a man who no longer loved her. With narrowed eyes, Diane focused on the road, determined to reach her destination in time. We'd been driving for six hours with only two stops in between. Apparently, time was of the essence. Not a minute could be wasted.

My oldest brother's father Sherman had recently left Diane to be with another woman. Day-in and day-out, I was forced to listen to my mother complain about how all of her love had been in vain. Sherman's abrupt absence had changed her, and therefore changing our lives in the process. Regardless of his infidelity, my mother wasn't ready to call it quits just yet. On a mission to reclaim what was rightfully hers, she headed to the city Sherman now called home. In the rearview mirror, I studied her reflection. I almost didn't recognize the woman sitting in the driver's seat. Sure, she looked like me with her deep caramel skin, high cheekbones, and chestnut eyes, yet her erratic behavior made me feel like she was a total stranger.

"Mommy," I whispered. "How much longer before we get there?" I asked as I rubbed my eyes.

"Just close your eyes, Mary," Diane told me, "Just close your eyes. And when you open them, we'll be where we're meant to be."

***

It was nearing 2 a.m. when we finally pulled into the cracked driveway of our great aunt's home. Big Mama resided in a rundown house, which looked like it should've been torn down years ago. An immediate sense of fear washed over me as I took in my surroundings. The neighborhood looked foreign. It was nothing like the place I knew as home. Automatically, I didn't like it there.

"Let's go," Diane said, opening the door. A cold gust of wind blew inside, immediately causing goose bumps to form on my arms.

Avon, my older brother, anxiously hopped out whereas I hesitated a little.

"I don't wanna," I rebutted.

Diane's head swiveled so hard she nearly gave herself whiplash. "I said let's go," she hissed. The sinister look in her dark eyes showed that she refused to be challenged. Reluctantly, I climbed out and walked behind my family towards the small house. I knew at that moment life wasn't going to be sweet.

***

Big Mama was my mother's supposed savior. In exchange for being taken care of, she granted us shelter in her three-bedroom, roach infested house. At 5'7 and three-hundred pounds, she was a burly, grouchy old woman unable to care for herself. For some strange reason she also could never get my name right. She addressed me by everything but Mary. When Big Mama wasn't busy getting my name wrong, she was yelling at my mother to do this and do that. Idly, I stood by and watched our great aunt ran her ragged. She did everything from cooking, and cleaning, to bathing Big Mama. And because her attention was needed in other areas, Diane slowly began to neglect me by the day.

As a child, I simply couldn't grasp the situation we were in. As far as I knew, we were happy in Cleveland. We didn't live in the nicest neighborhood or the fanciest house, but we were safe and content. There in Indiana, we were forced to adapt to our gloomy surroundings all in the name of love. The adoration Diane had for Sherman was quickly replaced with bitterness. When it was obvious that he wasn't coming back, she resorted to disrupting his new life the only way she knew how. Using me as the crutch, Diane suddenly placed me in beauty pageants just to compete with Sherman's new girlfriend's daughter.

    Fortunately, for me, the beauty pageant was one of the best things that ever happened to me. Initially, I was apprehensive about agreeing to it. After all, the only reason Diane had put me in the pageant was to provoke Katherine. Nevertheless, I loved the spotlight being on me regardless of my mother's hidden motives. At an early age, I knew right away that I wanted to be a star. In my opinion, the beauty pageants were the starting point in my life. I had one shot to prove to my mother and myself that I could be somebody special. But as expected, Diane's only concern was outshining Katherine. She figured competing with Sherman's new girlfriend was the only way to gain his attention.

    During my first contest, Diane went the extra mile to ensure that I was primped and pretty. With the last forty dollars she had left to our name, she bought me a cute baby blue leotard and white stockings to do my routine in. That was the most she'd done for me since we moved to Indiana. Staring at my reflection in the dressing room's vanity, I barely recognized the little girl gazing back at me. My mother stood behind me with a proud smile painted on her face. Deep down inside, I knew she was more pleased with herself than she was with me. For her, winning wasn't about a simple achievement. It was the only way she could get back at the woman who stole her life from right underneath her.

    "You look so beautiful," Diane said placing a heavily veined hand on my shoulder, "You've got this, Mary. I just know it." Glancing over her shoulder, she watched Katherine brush through her daughter's mid-length hair. "God will see to it that heathen's child doesn't win," she muttered.

    That day my mother got her wish. I walked off the stage wearing a ribbon, a crown, and a wide grin from ear-to-ear. I wanted her to be just as proud of me as I was of myself, but back in the dressing room, she couldn't wait to rub it in Katherine's face. Diane was so elated with my victory that I was tempted to hand her my crown.

"Are you done yet?" Katherine finally snapped on my mother. Her seven-year old daughter stood behind her with tears in her eyes.

Slowly Katherine approached Diane and stood face to face with her. "Your daughter won. Congratulations," she said smugly, "Too bad in the end, you still lost."

Katherine's comment immediately wiped the smirk off Diane's face. Whether she wanted to admit it not, the rude remark was the closure she desperately needed to finally let go. Sherman was never coming back.

***

For years, my mother and I lived under Big Mama's roof, abiding by her unjust rules. A little while after we arrived, my mother sent Avon off to live with his father leaving me to endure the struggles with my mother alone. In order to keep myself preoccupied at home, I began designing Barbie doll attire with scraps of clothing my aunt Tonya would give me. She was a thriving fashion designer, and I hoped to be just like her one day.

I also looked forward to the pageants Diane kept me in. And after numerous victories, Diane took an extra step to ensure that I would always win. Hesitantly, I agreed to wear a retainer in order to correct my "bunny teeth." She promised that it would make me prettier and set me apart from the other children in elementary school, so I happily obliged. Since kindergarten, I'd always loved school. It was the one thing I looked forward to each and every day. The one place I truly found solace. You couldn't pay me to miss a day. Every morning I woke up bright and early with my school clothes already laid out for the day. That was one responsibility Diane would never have to worry about. I'd also made it my mission to show up first to the bus stop, and the one time I did miss it, I nearly suffered an asthma attack chasing after the bus. School became my escape. Diane simply thought I was eager to learn. Though that was a part of the reason, I also relished being away from Big Mama's house. Since the day, we moved there, my life had been turned upside down, and Diane and I were now more distant than ever since she was always tending to her aunt. Things just weren't the same.

A normal day for me was seeing her once in the morning, on the way out the door, and again before, I went to sleep at night. As the days went by, my mother's appearance also changed. She'd lost a substantial amount of weight. Bags resided underneath her usually vibrant eyes. Big Mama was running Diane ragged with all her demands and requests. On the way down to Indiana, my mother had hope, but somewhere along the way she lost it, opting to settle with the life she naively chose instead. Most times at Big Mama's house, I kept myself preoccupied with music videos. I loved to see the various celebrities flash across the 14-inch television screen. Privately, I wondered about their journey to success, and if any of them once led lives similar to mine.

One day I'm gonna be famous, I promised myself.

"Mary," my mother yelled from the kitchen, "Come help me wash the dishes."

I turned off the television and stood to my feet. Seconds later, I joined Diane at the sink. A baby roach scurried past my foot and took refuge underneath the refrigerator. I didn't even flinch. By then, I was used to seeing them.

"I wash. You rinse and place them in the dish rack," she instructed.

At that moment, I became lost in my fantasy. *Long jet-black wavy hair flowed down my back as I sashayed across the stage. I wore a sparkling pearl white dress I had fashioned myself of course, and the latest pair of designer shoes. That night the Grammy Awards was filled to capacity with singers, rappers, and an array of famous actors and actresses. The walk to the podium felt so familiar. This was my third year winning the best female artist award. The handsome host passed me the microphone, so that I could give my brief speech. Staring out into the broad audience, I smiled in admiration.* "I just wanna thank my fans—"

"*Mary,*" *the host rudely cut me off,* "*Mary?*"

"Mary," Diane yelled snapping me back to reality, "You're letting the water run everywhere. Pay attention."

"Sorry," I murmured.

From the kitchen, I could hear Big Mama fussing for someone to come to her aid. Through my peripheral vision, I saw the frustration all over my mother's weary face. That was usually the norm for Big Mama. No matter what you were doing, she expected you to stop and help with whatever she needed. Scraping the blackness off a cast iron skillet with a knife, I was wise enough to keep quiet. I knew with anything I said, I was liable to be scolded. Diane's patience was nonexistent.

"I could've had so much more in life," she said more to herself than anyone else, "If I would've never had kids, I could've had so much more…"

"Diane," Big Mama continued to yell in the background.

My heart instantly sank to the pit of my stomach. Guilt consumed me causing me to believe that I was the reason for my mother's shortcomings. *Did she truly feel that way*? I wondered.

"Diane," Big Mama hollered.

"I'm coming," my mother screamed slamming the plate she was washing in the sink.

As she stomped off to tend to her aunt, tears filled my eyes before sliding down my cheeks. *She hates me*, I thought.

***

It was February of 1996 when Diane's mother passed away. The unexpected death took a heavy toll on her. If Sherman's departure wasn't enough, the loss of my grandmother was definitely the nail on the head. A few days before the memorial service, Diane and I drove back to Cleveland, Ohio. Unfortunately, it wasn't to return to our normal everyday lives. During the funeral, my mother suffered a nervous breakdown. Never in my life had I seen her so torn up inside. But the minute we got back to Indianapolis, things only got worse. The relationship I had with Diane became even more strained. Eventually, she completely let herself go. Half the time she stayed in her bedroom all day, so the cooking, cleaning, and taking care of Big Mama suddenly became my job.

Diane rarely, if ever, interacted with me, and the only time she showed care or concern was when beauty pageants were involved. No matter the circumstances, she never missed an opportunity to one-up Katherine. It was no longer about Sherman. Diane just loved to rain on her parade.

Because of the drastic change my mother underwent, my life continued to change as well. As the days carried on, I felt increasingly lonely; even school wasn't the safe haven it used to be. No longer did I anxiously run to the bus stop to make it to school on time.

A few weeks after my grandmother's death, I developed a nasty habit of stealing. I was so determined to cause others unhappiness that it didn't matter what I swiped. I stole everything from school supplies to the teacher's grading chart. The possessions held no value whatsoever and meant nothing to me. Half the stuff I couldn't even use. I didn't want anyone to have anything because I had nothing and no one. Unfortunately, my reign of terror only lasted for so long. Nearly a month after the funeral, my mother received a call from my teacher. She informed Diane that several of her items had come up missing and that I was the only student who sat close enough to her desk to take them. Later on that night, my mother discovered a trash bag filled to the brim with items I had stolen from school. Saying I was embarrassed would've been an understatement as my mother made me return everything the following morning. With her arms folded across her chest and a grim expression on her face, Diane watched as I dumped the contents of the trash bag in front of my entire class. I felt ashamed and angry with her for embarrassing me in such an outlandish way, and the snickers and whispers from my fellow students didn't help much either. At that moment, I felt lower than dirt. I couldn't believe Diane would do that to me. Like a dog with its tail tucked between its legs, I followed Diane out of the classroom. Over my shoulder, I could hear the teacher telling the class to settle down. From that moment, I hated my mother.

***

A few weeks after my little episode, I was surprised at school with a visit from Diane. Only this time it wasn't to make a mockery of me in front of my entire class. My mother pulled me out of school that day without so much as an excuse. She did things out of pure impulsiveness, and made hasty decisions that affected everyone's lives around her with no regard.

"Ma, why do I gotta leave?" I whined on the way to Big Mama's car. School was my refuge. Why on Earth would Diane strip me of my education? Typically, I never understood my mother's way of reasoning, but that decision seemed extremely out of character. Why was she taking the one thing I loved away from me?

"God spoke to me this morning and told me to save you from the condemned," she replied, "My eyes are finally open now. It all makes sense. The acting out. The stealing…"

"Ma, what are you talking about?" I refused to get in the car until she gave me a plausible reason.

"You're getting home schooled," Diane said matter-of-factly. She then pointed towards my school, "This place here is the devil!"

"Ma?"

"It is ungodly," she continued, "You're not learning anything. You need to learn what I teach you. They're poisoning your brain with worldly information."

"You can't take me outta school," I responded, "This isn't fair!"

"Get in the car, Mary," Diane said through clenched teeth. I could tell that she didn't appreciate me raising my voice.

"No."

"Mary!"

Without warning, I took off towards the busy street near the school.

"Mary?" my mother yelled after me.

My lungs burned from a lack of oxygen, but I didn't stop. Car tires screeched and drivers honked their horns as I ran through traffic hoping to get hit. Tears streamed down my cheeks and rolled off my chin before hitting onto the asphalt. Vehicles swerved around me, drivers desperate to evade a collision.

"Mary!" I could hear my mother screaming my name in the distance, but I couldn't stop.

SSSSSSCCCCCCCRRRRRRR!

Tears blurred my vision as I focused on the task at hand. For my ridiculous scene in front of my school, Diane punished me by making me pick the filth out of Big Mama's carpets. When I requested a broom, I was told that my hands would get the job done better. Diane was on her way upstairs when she stopped in mid-stride. In one hand was a white coffee mug and in the other was an aged bible. Anytime I saw those two items together, I knew she would be in her bedroom all day leaving me to do all the housework.

"The Lord said Honor thy mother and father and thy days will be longer. One of these days you gon' learn." Ignoring her blatant warning, I continued to pick food crumbs out of the worn out gray carpet.

For several months, my mother tried her best to home school me herself. Watching PBS became a regular routine. She also sent me off with an African friend to watch movies like *Sankofa*. I missed school with each day that passed, but anytime I mentioned it, I was immediately scolded. At that point, I didn't think my life would ever improve.

"Diane?" Big Mama called from her bedroom.

Sighing dejectedly, I turned the eye down on the stove. Tonight was the twelfth night in a row Ramen noodles would be for dinner. The meal, I didn't have an issue with. My only concern at the moment was my mother's whereabouts. Around noon, she left saying that she was going to the local library to get a few DVDs, but that was over ten hours ago.

"Diane?"

After draining the noodles, I placed the pot back on the stove and headed upstairs to tend to my aunt. I found Big Mama in her bedroom, which reeked of mildew. The larger window beside her dresser was covered with a tattered plaid sheet, which made the room dark.

"Yes, ma'am?" I answered standing in the doorway.

Big Mama stared at me with disdain. At times, I couldn't decipher whether she liked me or hated me.

"Diane ain't here yet?" she asked.

"No, ma'am," I answered in a small voice.

Big Mama's tiny eyes resembled two black marbles as she studied me. From where I stood, I could see the television reflecting off her lenses.

"I need you to put some Jheri juice in my hair," she finally said.

I didn't know how much glossier Big Mama's hair could get. Usually that was my mother's responsibility, but since her departure, I was stuck doing it. I was just about to fulfill Big Mama's request when I heard the front door open downstairs.

"Mary?" Diane called out, "Mary, come downstairs now."

Immediately, I ran to the kitchen where I found my mother moving about frantically. "Pack your stuff," she ordered, "We're leaving tonight."

Confusion swept across my face. For a second, I thought my ears were deceiving me. We'd been at Big Mama's house for years with no plans of ever relocating.

"Where are we going?"

"I met a man today. God brought him to me." Diane exclaimed walking hastily to her bedroom.

I followed behind her hoping for a better explanation. "Mama, who are you talking about?"

"Dr. J, sweetheart. He's our savior."

From the doorway, I watched my mother snatch clothes out of the mahogany dresser we had been using. After grabbing her necessities, she tossed them inside a backpack.

"Don't just stand there, Mary. Get to packing," she ordered.

Waiting for my mother and I on the porch was a tall, brown-skinned, neatly dressed man. His hair was cut low, nearly bald. He looked nice enough, but I was unsure about him being our "savior."

"Mary, this is Dr. J. Dr. J, this is my daughter Mary." Diane's introduction was rushed. I could tell that she was anxious to get far away from Big Mama's house. For the past few months, they'd bumped heads more than usual. However, I didn't think it had gotten that bad. "Mary, Dr. J was nice enough to offer to take us in," she explained, "God told me to take this path, so I am."

After leaving Big Mama's house, the hike to our destination was long and grueling. Since neither Dr. J nor Diane had a car, we were forced to travel by foot. It was nearing 11 p.m., and I was desperately battling sleep. I wanted to be in bed, but yet once again, I was being uprooted from a life I had grown accustomed to, and I couldn't understand why.

"Ma, can you please tell me where we're going?"

"We're going to someplace better," Diane simply said, "I'd rather be homeless than live in a house with that nagging woman."

Homeless? I thought. Big Mama's wasn't the best, but we had food and shelter. We didn't even know Dr. J. Sure, he dressed nice, but who was to say he could be trusted? Foolishly, I believed that he was taking us to some mansion or fancy home, but Dr. J led us to the last place I expected to be, an abandoned Big Boy restaurant. Together we entered through the back door, and I could see nothing but darkness as we quietly maneuvered.

"I have to pee," I whispered. The journey there had been so long that I found myself holding it.

"I'll show her to the bathroom," Dr. J volunteered.

Diane nodded her head in agreement. Hesitantly, I followed him down a dark hallway that led to the public bathroom. It wasn't until I walked in that I noticed there were no lights or running water, so I quickly did my business, and discovered I couldn't flush the toilet afterward. Afraid, I hurried back to my mother in the dining area. "Is this where we're gonna live?" I asked confused as ever.

"It's just temporary," Diane said, "Every struggle the Lord takes us through is just temporary."

2

"Every Flower Grows Through Dirt..."

Dr. J was once a wealthy entrepreneur who made his money by investing in the restaurant business. Purchasing the diner was the best move he'd ever made in his life. Sadly, his good fortune soon ran out after his wife left him and took every penny he had for herself. The only thing he was left with was his restaurant, but now it belonged to the bank. Luckily, Dr. J still owned a set of spare keys. The Big Boy restaurant was the temporary residence he'd extended to us. Although it was temporary, not having lights or running water felt inhumane. During our first night there, Dr. J taught me how to sleep with the blankets over my face so that I wouldn't get cold as I laid in one of the booths. It was a small trick he used to keep the air from getting in. Even though I was warm and snug, it was still hard to sleep with the jarring sound of rusted pipes rattling throughout the night. The public restrooms reeked because of the accumulated waste, but once every blue moon, Dr. J would dump a bucket of water down each stall to flush out its contents.

In order to cope with my new life, I would envision all the celebs that sat in the same booth I was sleeping on. In reality, I knew they would probably never step foot in the place; however, it felt good to dream.

***

For four months, Diane and I lived alongside Dr. J in the deserted diner. We ate continental breakfast, cleaned ourselves, and did our laundry at the hotel across the street. Every morning, Dr. J would scold me about not blending in. Apparently, he thought I looked too suspicious whenever we stepped foot inside. "Stop looking like that," he would say, "You need to look like you know what you're doing."

In order to keep suspicions down, we hid our belongings in an open ceiling tile. It wasn't the best living condition, but we did what we could to get by. Dr. J turned to not be that bad after all despite his situation. He was the one who instilled in me that no matter what my circumstances were, never let other people know. That was the primary reason why he still dressed flashy even though he was homeless. Sadly, I wore the same tattered clothes every day. The mirror in the bathroom of the restaurant was a painful reminder of our reality. After a while, I stopped looking at my reflection. I got tired of being disappointed with what I saw every time.

Diane ended up getting a job at a local Sam's Club as a cashier. Because we didn't have a phone, our family couldn't get in touch with us. No one knew our whereabouts as we kept a low profile in the closed down establishment.

***

"Diane. Mary," Dr. J whispered as he lightly shook my shoulder.

Diane and I woke up and wiped the sleep from our eyes.

"What's going on?" my mother grumbled.

"*Sshhhh*," Dr. J held his index finger to his lips.

Through the dirty restaurant windows, we could see the flashing blue and red lights out front. Evidently, the police had finally caught on to us living there.

"I need you two to leave out the back door," he said in a hush tone, "And please be as quiet as you can. I'll try to talk to them."

My mother and I quickly did as we were told. My heart thumped rapidly in my chest as I waited for what felt like forever. I didn't understand what was happening. Were we going to get in trouble?

"Mommy, what's…"

"Sshhhh," Diane hissed pressing her ear harder against the door to listen, "If you don't wanna go to jail, be quiet."

In silence, Diane and I listened to the police explain to Dr. J about the many phone calls they received about suspicious activity at the diner. They even looked around the building to see if the rumors were true about someone living there. Fortunately, Dr. J negotiated his way out of being arrested. Cutting him some slack, the police took his keys instead of taking him in. However, he was instructed to get his belongings and leave the premises immediately. After the cops pulled off, we quickly collected everything we owned and tossed it in black trash bags. Once we were all packed up, we left the building and started our journey down the railroad tracks behind the restaurant. Along the way, we found an unused train compartment where we stashed the bags.

Afterwards, we headed to the hotel across the street from the Big Boy to figure out our next move.

"Great," Diane complained, "Where are we gonna stay now?"

"This is your fault," Dr. J said to me, "If the police would've never seen the pee you left behind in the toilet, they would've never known someone was living there."

My heart instantly sank to the pit of my stomach. Guilt washed over me as he continued to chastise me. Lately it seemed like I could never do anything right. I opened my mouth to apologize, but all that came out was a low-pitched squeal. Tears pooled in my eyes as I looked up at Diane. Her expression showed that she was just as disappointed in me as Dr. J was.

"What are we gonna do now?" she asked. As usual, she looked to him for answers.

"Let me make a few phone calls," Dr. J told her, "I'll see what I can do."

I ended up falling asleep while waiting for them to come to a resolution. A woman who used to clean Dr. J's pools at his mansion was the person he ended up calling for assistance. Reluctantly, Susan agreed to let us temporarily stay in her office at work. After walking for what felt like an eternity, we finally arrived at a massive warehouse. Susan met us in front of the building with a smug expression on her face. The sashes around her pea coat were tied tightly. It was cold outside due to the season, and she didn't look too thrilled with being woken up in the middle of the night.

"Hey, Susan, I really appreciate you coming out. I know it's pretty late." He turned towards Diane and me. "This is…"

"Let's hurry up and get inside before we catch a cold," Susan said quickly cutting him off. It didn't take a rocket scientist to figure out that she didn't care who we were.

The three of us followed Susan inside where we were led to an office in the rear of the building. In the 12 x 12 office was a pull out bed, a space heater, and a real bathroom. A slow smile spread across my face.

"Now this can only be temporary," Susan stressed, "I mean it."

The Icing On Top Ain't Always Sweet

Dr. J nodded his head vigorously, "Totally understandable. Thank you, Susan for everything."

Without saying another word, she rushed out the office leaving us alone. Immediately, I ran inside the bathroom and turned on the sink's faucet letting the warm water soothe my skin.

***

The office was a major upgrade from the diner though it was not the home I longed for. At least there, I was able to bath versus having to wash in the sinks of the hotel. Every day Susan made it her business to remind us that we weren't permanent guests. I knew it would only be a matter of time before we had to return to the streets. Because of the underprivileged life I lived, I lost touch with being a child. I missed school, my friends, and my old neighborhood.

Every morning my mother asked Dr. J the same question over and over, "Where are we gonna go now?" He never had an answer. His options were just as limited as hers were. Over time, I could see the love and respect my mother had for Dr. J disappearing. She'd put her trust in him believing he would look out for us. Unfortunately, he had failed. Diane's disposition clearly showed that she didn't want to be around him anymore, but she didn't have much of a choice since she knew we couldn't go back to Big Mama's.

***

A few days after living in Susan's office, my mother took me with her to pick up her last check from Sam's Club. Since the location of her job was too far, Diane was forced to quit. Because we didn't have money for bus transportation, my mother and I rode bicycles. The ride there took more than three hours, and I suffered an asthma attack in between, so I was furious when I discovered the check was only sixty-four dollars.

"Ma, where are we gonna stay after Sarah kicks us out?" I asked on the way back. Every few minutes, I rotated between walking and riding the bike. Diane had suggested I do it that way, so I wouldn't have another attack.

"You don't know she's gonna kick us out," my mother said, "The devil makes us doubt. You just be quiet and roll with punches. You hear me?"

Sighing deeply, I muttered, "Yes, ma."

***

For days, we penny-pinched off Diane's last check using the money for only food and necessities. And just three weeks later, Susan informed us that our time was up.

"You've gotten too comfortable," she told Dr. J.

"Come on, Susan, please. All we need is a little time," he pleaded, "Just give us a bit more. We have nowhere else to go."

"Do you know how embarrassing it is for my employees to see you walking around here in your pajamas?" she countered, "I told you a few days. You've been here for weeks. I'm sorry, Dr. J, but you all have to go." Susan's gaze lingered on me for several seconds. Her blue eyes were sympathetic, but her tone was firm. "I need my office back," she said with finality.

I would never forget the look of desperation in Dr. J's eyes. Not only had he let Diane and I down, but also he'd let himself down too. Sarah was his last resort, and he had yet to find us another place to live. Dr. J clasped his hands together as if he were praying. "Susan, please, we have nowhere else to go. We have a child."

"I need you to get your things and leave before I call the police." The no-nonsense expression on her face showed that she wasn't kidding. We had overstayed our welcome.

"Let's go," Diane whispered placing her hand on Dr. J's shoulder. Thankfully, she was the voice of reason.

"Okay," Dr. J finally agreed, "We're leaving."

In silence, we collected our belongings and left the premises before Susan notified the authorities. Dragging our bags of clothes down a dimly lit street, I prepared for more hardships to come.

After leaving Susan's office, Diane and I ended up at Aunt Genie's house as a last resort. She was my mother's lively younger sister. Of course, Diane didn't agree with her wild lifestyle, so she only picked up the phone to call out of pure desperation. We only stayed there for a week, but words couldn't express how good it felt to sleep in a house again. Aunt Genie resembled a more youthful looking Diane. With her wide, vibrant eyes and high cheekbones, she was a reflection of what my mother used to look like before life hit. Many years ago, Genie came out as a lesbian further pushing my mother away. Diane, the ever bible toting tyrant, couldn't understand her decision, so she intentionally stayed away. Aunt Cheryl, Genie's girlfriend, was a sweet, mild-mannered woman with a daughter named Sherita, and she happily took me in with open arms. In the beginning, Diane was a bit hesitant to the idea of sending me off to live with someone else. However, all it took was a little convincing from Genie to get my mother to finally agree. Diane knew she was at a breaking point. With all of her options exhausted, she reluctantly agreed. Sherita's household best suited the living conditions I needed. Since she had two young kids of her own, I would finally be able to be around other children. I also wouldn't have to worry about where we would sleep the next night.

  I would never forget the day Diane and I went our separate ways. She rejoined Dr. J on the streets in a quest to find their new home, and I went with Sherita. In the end, I knew it was for the best.

***

  Sherita was a young single mom with two kids. She worked two jobs in order to provide for her family. The reason she was willingly to take me in was because she didn't want to see me homeless and she also could've used a little extra help with her children. Because I was much older, I was able to baby sit and do household chores when she needed it.

  The first day living with Sherita, she ridiculed my clothing and bland hairstyle, so the next morning she took me to Target and bought me new wardrobe. I felt like I was on a shopping spree as I grabbed the cutest colored outfits I could find and tossed them in the cart. After upgrading my wardrobe, Sherita helped me get back into school. I had been out for a year and a half due to my situation with my mother. Sherita made sure to tell the principal everything I'd gone through, but despite my situation, I was held back a grade because of my late return. Nevertheless, I was just glad to be going back to school. The school Sherita placed me in was unlike any other public school I had ever attended, but thankfully, it wasn't hard fitting in and building friendships. I couldn't have asked for a better environment.

Living with Sherita restored my confidence again. She taught me how to keep up with my physical appearance and covered the things I needed to know about coming into my womanhood. Sherita treated me as if I were her own daughter. Anything she did for her two sons, she did for me as well. Anytime she yelled at them, she yelled at me too. She treated all of us equally and never made me feel any differently. During the hours she worked, I was left home to baby sit, but it was the most enjoyable part of my life. I loved Kylan and Keenan as if they were my own siblings and took care of them as such.

All went well for the first few weeks until the evening I made a dreadful mistake. Sherita had left me home alone with the kids one evening for a few hours. Her new boyfriend was supposed to be coming back with her, and she wanted the house to be in order.

"I just need you to put the dishes in the dishwasher," she told me over the phone, "After that you can go to sleep. I should be home by 11 p.m."

"Okay, I'll do it now," I eagerly said. Anxious to show that I could be responsible, I didn't want to give her any reason to send me away. The last thing I wanted was to end up back on the streets with Diane and Dr. J.

"Thank you, sweetie. See you in the morning."

After disconnecting the call, I raced into the kitchen and grabbed the dishwashing liquid off the counter. Once I piled every last dirty dish into the dishwasher, I poured the blue liquid all over them. Finally, I closed the door and started the machine.

***

"Mary? Oh my God, Mary, what did you do?"

Sherita's high-pitched yells awoke me that night. Instantly, I jumped out the bed and ran into the living room where I slid into a huge pile of bubbles.

"Mary, what did you do?" Sherita hollered. She could barely navigate through the house filled with the soapsuds.

Suddenly, Sherita's children appeared in the room. Their small eyes widened in disbelief at the sight before them. Without warning, I broke into soft sobs. I just knew that was it for me. I was positive that Sherita was going to send me away.

Fortunately, Sherita didn't kick me out after my little incident. No television for the entire next day was the punishment for my crime. I loved living with Sherita, and I looked up to her as a role model. As a single mother working two jobs, she was very admirable. With chocolate skin, short hair, and a nice curvy figure, Sherita was the epitome of a strong-willed woman to me. She had her own place, kept up her appearance, and pushed a fly car that I hoped she'd pass down to me one day. Life with Sherita really helped mold me into the young lady I was becoming.

Aside from being back in school, what I loved most of all was being able to have a normal life again. No longer did I have to walk around in the same old tattered clothes. Sherita made sure I had the nicest things she could afford. Soon after moving in with her, I resumed writing poetry and music again. A happier life had ignited the flame that went out during my homeless stint. After getting back in the groove of things, I started a small music group with a couple other girls in my elementary school. During my recreational time, we would sing and perform in my living room to the songs we wrote ourselves. It was nice to finally be happy, and I couldn't have asked for a better life. Unfortunately, it was only a matter of time before Diane weaseled her way back in my life causing conflicting issues into the process.

For my upcoming eleventh birthday, Sherita had decided to throw me a special party. I was amazed at the extra mile she had went to ensure that I enjoyed my special day. I'd never had a birthday party before, so the gesture alone meant a lot to me. For my birthday weekend, I was allowed to have a few friends over from school for a sleepover. That Friday evening everyone carpooled to the new IMAX Theater where I'd be seeing my first 3-D movie. Words couldn't express how excited I was, yet somehow Diane found a way to make my day about her. In the beginning, it started out with her being upset that I didn't ride to the movies with her. Instead, I had opted to cruise along with my friends. Then through the entire movie, she acted uneasy because I chose to sit with them in the theater. Whenever I stole a glance in Diane's direction, I saw the unhappiness all over her face. Secretly, I knew that she was bitter about not being able to afford to give me a birthday herself and resented the fact that I became close with Sherita.

Once the movie ended, and we returned home, I was barely able to enjoy my birthday weekend with my mother's incessant calling and nagging. Sherita had to temporarily block Diane's number just to get a peace of mind. It was all rather confusing to me considering this was the most concern she'd shown me in years. In all honesty, she was simply envious of the relationship I'd grown to have with Sherita. Her taking me in was supposed to be a favor, but now Diane felt as if Sherita were stepping on her toes. And truth be told, Sherita was far from being my mother's biggest fan. Still, I tried my best to enjoy myself especially since Sherita had gone over and beyond for me. After an exciting night filled with friends, family, and fun, I was awakened the following morning by the sound of loud knocks on the patio door. My eyes shot open when I saw the silhouette of a person standing out on the patio. My friends and I had made pallets and slept on the living room floor, so I quietly walked over to see who it was. We lived on the third floor, so whoever was on the opposite side of the door had to climb up three floors. After wiping the sleep from my eyes, I recognized who it was. It was Diane.

"Oh, my goodness," I mumbled in disbelief. I continued to tiptoe to the door that led to the patio. "Ma, what are you doing out here?" I asked.

"I've been calling you like crazy," she explained. As expected, Diane was winded from the workout she'd just endured. Worry lines creased her face, and I almost didn't recognize her. I was surprised that I didn't see Dr. J lurking over her shoulder. I wanted to ask if she were still sticking it out with him, but I decided against it.

"I've been worried sick about you," she said tilting my head from side to side as if she were examining me for bruises, "The Lord is my witness I called Sherita a total of twenty-seven times. Why is she purposely ignoring me?" Diane demanded to know.

"Because I'm fine," I assured her, "As you can clearly see."

Diane's eyes narrowed. She wasn't used to sarcasm especially from me. "A hard life might've aged you a few years, but you're still a child, and I am still your mother," she reminded me, "Sherita's got you spoiled, I see." Diane said her name as if venom was on her tongue. "Enjoy it while it lasts because this is only temporary."

3

"Train your mind to see the good in every situation..."

Six months after living with Sherita, I began to experience excruciating pain in my mouth caused by the retainer I still wore. Apparently, my mother was supposed to have it removed over a year ago. Unfortunately, homelessness and a nervous breakdown distracted her from her priorities. One morning, the pain was so unbearable that I thought my jaw had broken in my sleep. Stumbling inside the small bathroom, gripping my face, I made way to the sink and looked in the mirror. For quite some time, I'd known that my mouth had outgrown the retainer. But since it wasn't causing any discomfort, I decided against speaking up, but now things were different. Luckily, the following morning I got my wish. Instead of an orthodontist being the one to remove it, the retainer had fallen out on its own, but due to me over wearing it, the retainer caused an under bite. Initially, I didn't notice the change in my appearance until the day my art class was instructed to draw each other's silhouettes. Evidently, Kevin, my partner, found it humorous to draw a seemingly distorted portrait of me from the side.

"That is not how I look," I said snatching the Manila paper from him.

"Hey, I'm just drawing what I see," he replied nonchalantly.

I was so angry at his depiction of me that I balled the drawing up and threw it on the floor.

"What did you do that for," he snapped.

"Because that's not how I look!"

Our art instructor quickly came over to tend to the altercation, but I dismissed myself before she even said a word to me. Later on that day when I got home, I took a picture of myself in the mirror from the side. It wasn't until then that I realized Kevin's drawing of me was accurate. Wearing the retainer longer than needed had caused an under bite that once never existed. Tears pooled in my eyes as resentment filled my heart. *Diane promised the retainer would make me pretty*, I thought bitterly.

***

For the entire fourth and fifth grade, I lived with Sherita. Over time, she and Cheryl had become like second mothers to me. They taught me about femininity and always offered helpful advice whenever I needed it. Sherita also helped me to rebuild confidence in myself even with the new under bite I had developed. I loved the new life I had built with them, but as they say, *nothing lasts forever*.

During the summer before sixth grade began, Diane moved Avon and me back in with her after finally getting on her feet. She rented a cozy three-bedroom apartment in an urban area of Indianapolis. Although, I was sad to leave Sherita and her sons, I was grateful to have a chance to start over with my mother. Of course, the transition was tough, and for the first few weeks, I went back and forth between spending some nights at my mother's but most at Sherita's. I barely got a chance to settle in good before Dr. J wandered onto our doorstep. What I wasn't anticipating was my mother giving him my bedroom forcing me to sleep on the worn out sofa in the living room. I didn't have much of a choice, so I just went with it. Eventually, I got tired of being woken up every time someone entered the room. I didn't have the slightest ounce of privacy, and at my age, I desperately needed my own room.

Taking it upon myself, I made the downstairs bathroom my sanctuary. Avon called me crazy when he saw me making the tub into my own personal bed. I'd even gone as far as to put a sign on the outside of the door, which read *Mary's Room*. Fortunately, everyone in the house respected me enough to never use the bathroom, so it became my hideout from the world whether anyone understood it or not. Every day Diane scolded me about returning to the sofa, but I needed my own space. We barely lived in the townhome for two months before my mother was evicted. Dr. J went his separate way while we found another place in the heart of downtown Indianapolis. Diane moved us into section-8 housing and enrolled me in the nearest middle school. It was a far cry from the awesome school Sherita had placed me in, but beggars couldn't be choosers. There I made a couple of friends who shared the same passion for music as I did. Vashawn was a pretty, dark-skinned girl, with a curvy figure for her young age. She was also one of the most popular girls in school. Erica, like me, was in the 4-foot club and rather slender in frame. Vashawn, Erica, and I formed a music group where we performed at talent shows, school events, and any local place that allowed us to. After recording the songs on our karaoke machine, we passed the tapes out all over the city to spread our name. Since Diane wouldn't allow me to spend the night at anyone's house, me and my girls did most of our recordings at my house. We tried to do as many shows as possible to boost awareness. My first performance with them, though a small one, was a major milestone in my life that would forever remain etched in my mind. Five minutes before show time, I felt a combination of anxiousness, nervousness, and excitement. It had been years since I performed, but I knew in my heart that I was born to be somebody. The moment I stepped onto the stage with my girls was amazing. It felt like pure euphoria. Adrenaline pumped through my veins as I grabbed the microphone. It was finally my moment to shine. I knew then that I would never let anything hinder my dreams again because Vashawn, Erica, and I were headed to straight to the top. Forming the music group was the best thing that happened to me since the beauty pageants. Only this was for me, and not some silly revenge Diane was set on getting. I was finally living my dream, and it felt good to be surrounded by likeminded individuals. In school, I was recognized as the small girl with a big voice. Although I wasn't the most popular, like Vashawn, I was admired for my talent, well everyone except, Crystal Alexander my first childhood bully.

    Crystal had no real reason for disliking me other than the fact that I always got the lead roles in choir. At 5'10, she towered over me by an entire foot. Still, that never stopped her from teasing and taunting me every chance she got. The bullying lasted three long months until one afternoon when she caught me in the restroom alone.

    "I saw you come in here, Mary," Crystal said pounding on the stall's closed door. I was halfway through finishing my business when she unexpectedly caught me off guard. "You can't stay in there forever," she taunted, "At one point or another, you gotta come out."

    Sighing in frustration, I flushed the toilet and waited in silence for several seconds. I hoped and prayed that she would just leave me alone, so I could get on with my day, but as expected, she did the opposite.

Why me? I asked myself.

Even though I tussled with my brothers from time to time, I wasn't one that liked to fight. Diane had always stressed that ladies didn't fight.

She isn't really going to hit you, I tried to convince myself before finally opening the stall door.

Crystal loomed over me like a predator stalking its prey. "I see the way you be looking at me and stuff. You got something you wanna say?"

I tried my best to ignore her weak attempt at provoking me as I continued to wash my hands.

"Hello? Do you hear me talking to you, little girl?" she hollered.

"I don't know about you," I said drying my hands off, "But I'm going back to gym class." I made a move towards the exit but was suddenly blocked by Crystal's burly frame. Before I could do anything, she grabbed and slammed me forcefully against the bathroom mirror. It immediately shattered upon impact. From the crazed look in her eyes, I could tell that she hated me. There wasn't a single person in the bathroom, so she wasn't doing it for the attention. Her dislike for me was personal.

Using all of the strength I was able to muster up, I drew back and kicked Crystal as hard as I could. She instantly flew into the stall I had just exited moments earlier. Before she could get up, I made a daring attempt to leave the restroom, but she caught me off guard when she lunged at me full force. Together we tussled on the dirty tile floor, and some way, somehow, I was able to climb on top of her. Filled with rage, I grabbed her head and banged it against the porcelain toilet several times. Crystal's arms flailed wildly, but I refused to let up. She'd easily become a victim of my pent up frustration after her constant torture.

"Are you gonna leave me alone if I let you up?" I asked lightening the pressure I had on her head just a little.

"I'm gonna make you pay when I get up," she screamed.

Apparently, she wasn't in the mood to negotiate. With no other options left, I knew I would have to make a run for it. Keeping

Crystal's head pressed firmly on the toilet, I silently counted down to five. Her arms continued to thrash around wildly.

On the count of two, I bolted out of the stall and raced back to class. When I finally made it there, everyone was in attendance but Crystal. Using her absence to my advantage, I told anyone that would listen about the fight. Unfortunately, our gym instructor wasn't present. As usual, Mr. Arenas was running tardy, so I rattled off the details to my fellow students who immediately sympathized with me. Due to my small stature, they automatically felt like the fight wasn't fair because of our obvious height difference. Suddenly, in a fit of rage, Crystal stormed inside the gym. Her red-rimmed eyes focused in me from across the room.

"Little girl, I'm gonna kill you!" she screamed charging at me full-speed.

In an attempt to give me an advantage, one of the girls helped me onto the nearby bench where I posted up to fight. All it took was one uncoordinated swing from Crystal to knock me clean off the bench. As if on cue, the gym instructor raced towards us and broke up the fight. He then briskly led us to the principal's office where we were both suspended and arrested on sight.

***

"I am so disappointed and upset with you!" Diane grilled me the moment I climbed into the car. She had just picked me up from the juvenile detention center, and judging from her expression, I could tell that she wasn't at all pleased.

"But I was only defending myself," I said in a small voice, "None of this would've ever happened if Crystal had never put her claws on me. What was I supposed to do?"

Ironically, Crystal and I had befriended each other in the short amount of time we were locked up together. Upon intake, I was ordered to remove my weave before entering a holding cell. Apparently, Crystal took pity on my disheveled appearance and offered to braid my hair for me. During the brief encounter, she revealed where her hatred for me stemmed from. She was upset that I took lead in choir. She felt the position should've been hers from the beginning. It was all rather immature and foolish. Nevertheless, I was relieved that we could put our differences aside.

"The Lord's children don't need to defend themselves," Diane said snapping me from my thoughts, "For they know God fights all their battles."

I rolled my eyes at my mother's never-ending preaching. She was the biggest hypocrite I knew.

"You're on punishment too," Diane added, "And I have an assignment for you when we get back home. You got another thing coming if you think you're about to kick back and relax like you're on break. No, you're gonna learn, little girl."

Later that day, Diane had given me the seemingly impossible task of reading the Bible from Genesis all the way to Revelations. She claimed that familiarizing myself with the Word was the only way to cleanse myself. Never the trouble-making type, my mother could not understand my newfound behavior. Unfortunately, a few scripts from the Bible didn't stop my short-lived reign of terror.

After my encounter with Crystal, I found myself in a series of fistfights and other altercations. No longer would I tolerate being picked on and tormented. If I had to beat the respect out of my fellow classmates to gain it then that's exactly what I planned to do.

One Thursday afternoon I found myself being teased about my under bite on the school bus. Usually, I'd be the first one to post up in order to settle matters. However, my aggressor was a boy. Doing something I hadn't done in a while, I resorted to ignoring him. Unfortunately, that only lasted for so long. Fed up with the constant teasing, I hopped out my seat and jumped in the overgrown boy's face. I was so close to him that I could see the whiteheads on the tip of his nose.

"You won't have much to say after I punch you in the face," I said.

With a menacing stare, my contender stepped closer to me. He was so tall that I nearly reached his belly button. "What did you say me?" he asked through clenched teeth.

My heart sank to the pit of my stomach. Suddenly, I didn't feel so bold.

Without warning, a tall, light-skinned boy I only recognized from the basketball team rushed to my rescue. Gently moving me to the side, he stepped in the burly boy's face. "Hey, leave her alone, man."

"Or what?" the bully challenged.

As the boy stepped closer, their foreheads were practically touching. "Or else you'll have to deal with me. And trust me, you don't want that."

The bully continued to stand his ground, but judging from his expression I could see that he was mulling over the ultimatum. "Whatever," he finally said before walking off.

It felt good to release the breath I had been holding in the whole time. "Thank you," I whispered.

My hero slowly turned around to face me, and I was able to get a good look at him. He was absolutely gorgeous. With his creamy skin, fresh cornrows, and hazel eyes, I knew he was far out of my league. Still, that didn't stop me from silently admiring him.

"No problem," he smiled revealing his cute set of dimples, "I'm Devin, by the way."

I opened my mouth to reveal my name, but nothing came out. Shyness consumed me as I stared at him nervously. All of a sudden, the bus shifted as it turned, and I fell right into Devin's arms. "Whoa, are you okay?" he asked.

Like a scared little girl, I quickly broke away and rushed to the back of the bus. At only twelve, I had no experience whatsoever with boys. And if it was up to Diane, I probably wouldn't for another twenty years. After sliding in a seat beside a quiet girl with glasses, I felt myself blushing.

Devin, I repeated to myself. I had found my first school crush.

The following afternoon, my eyes scanned the huge cafeteria in search of Devin. I found him seated at a table with his fellow teammates and a few cheerleaders. In the beginning, I felt foolish for approaching him, but there was a part of me that felt obligated to properly thank him. The moment I reached Devin's table, everyone immediately stopped talking, and a few of the girls rolled their eyes.

"Hey, Devin, right?" I asked smiling.

He grinned and nodded his head at me. "I never got your name."

"Mary," I eagerly answered, "I—I didn't get a chance to thank you for standing up for me on the bus."

"Any time," he smiled.

The Icing On Top Ain't Always Sweet

My cheeks flushed red, and I quickly turned around and walked away to avoid Devin seeing it. I could hear a few of the cheerleaders giggle behind me, but I didn't care. I was on cloud nine. And seeing the type of girls he surrounded himself with suddenly gave me an idea.

***

"What do you mean you wanna be a cheerleader?" Diane asked with a frown.

After offering to help her with the dishes, I slowly tried to gage my mother's reaction to the idea. "Ma, I really think this could be good for me."

"Good? How? By wearing some short skirt and prancing around like a little fast girl."

"Cheerleading is not for fast girls, Ma."

"Let me think about it."

"But, Ma?"

"I said let me think about it," Diane repeated sternly.

With no other choice, I dropped the subject. I could only hope and pray that my mother eventually came around to the idea.

But an approval from Diane was harder to get than a letter of acceptance from Harvard. Although it felt like it took a century for her to finally give in, I was just happy when she actually agreed. The following morning after I was given her blessing, I tried out for the cheerleading squad. Even though I was out of my element, I knew if I tried hard enough I'd make it. I had a passion for entertaining, and I knew how to hold a crowd's attention. Trying out for the cheerleading team reminded me of the beauty pageants I did as a child. Like the pageants, I had to compete against a group of other girls to determine who made the cut. When my turn finally came, I took a deep breath and counted down to five in my head. The room was filled with every popular girl in school. After swallowing my fear and apprehension, I pulled out my best tricks and splits to wow the judges. By the time I finished my forty-five second routine, everyone's mouth in the gym was open. Panting heavily, I tried my best to keep my poise while waiting for the final verdict.

***

"I did it, Ma! I did it!" I said running through the house in search of Diane.

She walked out into the living room with an irritated expression on her face and a worn out Bible in her right hand. Evidently, I had interrupted her reading.

"What did I tell you about yelling in the house?" she asked.

"I'm sorry, Ma, but I'm excited," I said in a more hushed tone, "I made the cheerleading squad!"

Diane's thin eyebrows rose in surprise. Almost as if, she didn't expect for me to make it. "Oh," she simply said.

A look of disappointment swept across my face. "Oh?" I repeated.

"What do you want me to say?" Diane asked heading towards the kitchen.

Tears stung my eyes as I watched my mother walk away. "I want you to be happy for me." With that, I headed for my bedroom. Diane could be so cold at times. *She never wants to see me in the spotlight unless it's shining on her too*, I convinced myself.

***

Regardless of my mother's rudeness, I enjoyed my newfound hobby. Cheerleading was an exciting escape for me. Devin and I had also gotten closer, but our relationship was more sibling-like than anything else. He affectionately called me his little sister, and I treated him like one of my brothers. I loved our friendship. Every weekend, I rode my bicycle to Devin's house, which was conveniently located at the end of my block. Together we sat on his porch talking and laughing while enjoying sodas and Hot Cheetos. We talked about everything under the sun, and I even found myself revealing intimate secrets. We had that type of bond. No one else bothered me since I had befriended Devin. As the best friend to the lead basketball player, people knew better than to disrespect me unless they wanted to deal with him. Because he looked out for me, I held the utmost respect and admiration for him. But just because Devin was my friend didn't mean a girl couldn't dream. Whenever *Maury* aired its popular *"From Geek to Chic"* episode, I would plop in front of the TV and fantasize about being on the show. Vivid scenes of me surprising Devin after I was all grown up flooded my mind.

One day, I reassured myself.

The Icing On Top Ain't Always Sweet

Upon building a friendship with Devin, I decided that it was time to get my life back on track. Of course, it took a little of his encouragement. Soon after my reawakening, Vashawn, Erica, and I reunited and continued to make music. The following summer, we finally got our big break.

A nearby church held a contest for local kids in order to keep them off the streets. That year's grand prize was $500. I just knew my girls and me had what it took to win especially since we had yet to lose a single contest. The moment Vashawn, Erica, and I registered, I made a silent pledge to myself to put my all into winning. In my heart, I believed the victory could lead to greater things for us, so every Saturday morning, I woke up bright and early to catch the church bus that would pick us up. My eyes lit up every time I saw the white and red vehicle turn the corner. Words could not express my excitement.

A few weeks later, I found out that I would be attending a different high school than the rest of my friends. Evidently, my middle school recommended that I attend Broadripple, a local performing arts academy. The gesture was sweet, but starting over again was not something I wanted to do.

"Sucks you're moving," Devin said one afternoon while we sat on his rickety porch swing.

"Yeah, tell me about it."

"You're gonna be okay," he said taking my hand in is.

Easy for him to say, I thought.

***

The day of the church competition felt like Christmas all over again. I eagerly woke up at the crack of dawn in order to get my day started early. Since Diane didn't have the funds to buy me an outfit, my aunt Genie graciously stepped up. With the money she had given me, I bought a cute pink outfit from Dollar General, which was all I could afford. After altering and adding my own touches to it, it was more than acceptable.

We're going to win this competition. I have no doubt in my mind, I told myself.

Looking over my reflection in the bathroom mirror, I was extremely pleased with what I saw as I played with the colorful braids that hung freely over my shoulders. During summer break, I volunteered at a local beauty supply store. In exchange for my services, the owner gave me all the braiding hair that didn't sell. As usual, I made the best of it, but eventually the hair grew on me. As a matter of fact, the colored hair actually added to my unique personality, and all I saw was success as I stared at my reflection.

Jogging down the stairs, I raced towards the front door and prepared to head out. You would've thought I'd just won the lottery from the way my eyes lit up after seeing the church bus pull. The driver did his signature three-honks to make his presence known.

"Ma, I'm leaving," I called out figuring that she was probably still in her bedroom. But to my surprise, Diane was up and cleaning the kitchen.

"Where are you going?" she asked as if she didn't know already know about the competition I bragged about on a daily basis.

"Ma, I told you already."

"You aren't going anywhere," she snarled.

It felt like my whole world came crashing down after hearing those devastating four words. My mother knew how important the competition was to me, so I didn't understand why she was suddenly giving me a hard time about it.

"Ma, what are you talking about? You knew about the competition. I've been telling you about it for weeks."

The church bus driver continued to honk the horn outside, but my feet stayed planted to the ground. Diane grabbed the broom and dustpan from the corner of the kitchen. She then made her way back over to me. "The Lord has other plans," she stated shoving the items into my hands.

My eyes burned from the oncoming tears that fell as I heard the bus finally pull off taking my dreams along with it. Tears continued to roll off my chin and dropped onto the warm cement as I swept the alley behind our home. My beautiful outfit was covered in dust, and my hair was a mess. *So much for winning a competition*, I thought. At that moment, I felt like the biggest loser in life. I had worked so hard to win the competition only for my mother to snatch the opportunity from right under me. Saying that I was devastated would've been an understatement.

"Eventually, not even Diane will be able to hold me back," I told myself.

***

I was grateful when the school year finally returned, so that I wouldn't have to look at Diane all day. The much-needed distance between us was a blessing. Diane had caused a permanent rift between us after ruining my chances of winning the church competition. We rarely spoke to her. But regardless of what was happening at home, I was excited to finally start high school. It felt like a whole new world. I didn't have any of my old friends there to keep me company. Nevertheless, I was happy to take on the new challenge. Besides, I would be taking dance and music, my two passions in life.

When school began, the first few days proved to be tougher than I imagined. The assignments were harder than that of my old school, and I could hardly keep up. Soon, I found myself cheating off a nearby student in English class just to get by. Chandi McMillan was a super smart fourteen-year old with fair skin and wide eyes. It didn't take a genius to know she purposely allowed me to steal glances. I just didn't know if she pitied my lack of knowledge or just wanted a friend. Two days later, I finally got my answer.

"Hey," Chandi greeted me with her books tightly clutched against her chest.

I stood in front of my locker with my colorful plaits setting me apart from everyone else. The bell hadn't even rung for class to begin yet, so I didn't know why she was speaking to me.

"Hey," I murmured, barely looking up to greet her.

"We should totally share lockers," she said struggling to make conversation, "I have a ton of extra space."

"Uh, thanks. I guess."

"Cool," Chandi smiled revealing her braces, "See you in class."

Little did I know that it was the start of a blossoming friendship.

4

"You will face many defeats in life...but never be defeated."

"Hey, how about we have a sleepover at your house?" Chandi asked as we strode home together after school. We'd quickly become good friends in a matter of weeks. Both of our birthdays were in May, and our personalities were completely in sync.

Chandi was soft-spoken and subtle with her appearance whereas I was more daring and unique with my wardrobe. We were complete opposites, but it was our obvious differences that fueled our friendship.

"My mother won't let me have sleepovers," I told her, "And you can forget about her letting me sleep over at your house."

Chandi nodded her head in agreement. "My mom's the same the way."

My eyebrows rose in curiosity because this was the first time she had ever mentioned her mother. Chandi never spoke about her home life. Although we were best friends, she kept that part of her life separate.

"Whatever," I shrugged changing the subject, "You coming to the game this weekend? It'll be my first time cheerleading at Broad."

Chandi hesitated a little as she chewed the inside of her lip, "We'll see," she said.

"Chandi, you know how important this is to me," I stressed.

"I know," she said, "And so is this upcoming English test, so let's hurry up and get to the library and study.

Thankfully, Chandi had agreed to tutor me after school. It felt good knowing I would no longer have to cheat off her papers. Not only that, but it was cool having a friend that was both smart and laid back. Chandi went to school for theater, whereas I went for music. She was the yin to my yang, and although we were different as night and day, we were very close. Chandi quickly became inseparable. She was the closest thing to a sister I had, and I treated her as such.

***

The Icing On Top Ain't Always Sweet

"Did you make your mind up yet?" I asked Chandi that Friday. There was one day left before the big game, and I really wanted her to be there. Besides, it wasn't as if Diane was coming to offer her motherly support. We were on our way to study hall, and I figured that was as good a time as any to ask again.

Chandi frowned. "I can't, Mary. I'm really sorry."

"What do you mean 'you can't'? It's Saturday. What else do you have planned?" I pressed.

"I—I have to help my mother with something. She's going through some stuff, and she needs me at home," Chandi stammered. She pushed her glasses up on the bridge of her nose, and tried her best to play it cool, but I knew there was something else up.

"Fine," I said dryly, "I understand. No big deal. It's only my first game here."

"There'll be others," Chandi smiled oblivious to- my blatant sarcasm.

"Yeah," I reluctantly agreed, "there will."

***

I was so upset and disappointed that Chandi couldn't make my game that I started avoiding her. Days quickly passed by since I'd spoken to her, which was strange considering we shared lockers and English class. Initially, I didn't think too much into Chandi's absence because I was mad at her. However, when day three finally rolled around, I grew nervous. It was unlike Chandi to miss school especially so many days in a row. On the fourth day, I finally put my pride aside and decided to call her. To my surprise, there was no answer. Using my resources, I called Pam Thomas, a girl who lived down the street from Chandi who always stayed up-to-date on all the latest gossip around school.

"Hey, have you seen Chandi around?" I asked, "She hasn't been to school the last few days, and I'm really starting to get worried."

"I haven't, but I do know there were a bunch of cop cars surrounding her house the other day."

The following morning, I had an awkward, inexplicable feeling. On the bus, everyone's eyes seemed to be focused on me. It was as if they knew something I didn't.

What the hell is going on? I asked myself.

When I finally got to school, the awkwardness increased even more. Students were eerily quiet. After reaching my locker, I noticed that Chandi's pink backpack wasn't inside. That only meant one thing; she hadn't returned to school yet. My suspicions grew even more, but I tried my best not to worry.

We'll talk soon and she'll tell me what's going on, I convinced myself.

After grabbing my textbooks from my locker, I headed to my English class. As I slid in my assigned seat, I stole a glance at Chandi's desk. As expected, it was emptier than her side of the locker. One by one, I watched my fellow students fill the classroom. They looked just as miserable as the students on the bus did, and the strange stares didn't stop. Finally, our teacher Mrs. Taylor entered the class with a somber expression. In one hand was a coffee mug and in the other was a newspaper.

"What's up with everybody? Ya'll not happy we won the game?" I asked the few students around me.

Mrs. Taylor placed her mug on her desk and walked over to me. Without uttering a single word, she handed me the newspaper. Tears immediately pooled in my eyes as I stared at Chandi's black and white picture. "*Mother Claims the Lives of Her Daughters before Taking Her Own.*"

***

Chandi's funeral was one of the saddest days of my life. The First Baptist Church was crammed to capacity with people from all over the city coming to pay their respects. The entire time during the memorial service, I felt a combination of anger and sorrow. Angry at the fact that Chandi's mother's casket was even present and sorrowful because I'd lost my best friend.

Why are they even showing her face like she wasn't the one who killed them? I thought.

Chandi's mother had shot her youngest daughter, and then Chandi before turning the gun on herself leaving behind a quickly scribbled suicide letter. She claimed that heaven was a better place for her children. Apparently, the stress of bills and finances drove her to have a nervous breakdown. Following the tragic event, the infamous suicide note was published and read regularly on the news station. They covered the devastating story so much that I'd completely given up on watching TV altogether. Life after Chandi's death wasn't the same for me. As quickly as I made a close friend, she was unexpectedly snatched away from me. I didn't understand how a person could harm a hair on an innocent child especially a mother.

Over the next few weeks, I completely shut down. I rarely, if ever, spoke and most of the time I just wanted to be alone. Never had a death hit so close to home, and I didn't know how to cope with the loss. Since Diane was unable to sympathize with my strange behavior, she stayed out of my way for the most part, which was fine by me. Like a girl trapped in a bubble, I shielded myself from society to deal with my friend's death. Things were rough, and I blamed myself for ever being angry with Chandi over something so minor. Unfortunately, I would never get the opportunity to apologize. Eventually, I began to dress like a tomboy, choosing baggy clothes and sneakers over my usual girly attire. I simply didn't have the energy or passion to dress up anymore, and honestly, I didn't care what people thought. In my past time, I wrote dark poetry as a means to vent. When that didn't seem to satisfy me, I began sending my father suicide letters while he was imprisoned. At that point, it felt like he was the only one able to save me from my pain.

My father Art McKoy and I had never had a close relationship due to the distance and his lack of attention. I resented that he never handled his fatherly duties while I was growing up, but now he had a chance to make everything right, a chance to rescue me. Since he was getting out soon, I hoped and prayed that he'd come and take me away. But despite my circumstances, I stuck with cheerleading. It was the only thing that made me feel normal. Besides, I felt like if I gave up, and I refused to let her down.

***

After a game ended one evening, one of the basketball players approached me in the hallway. We were the only two in the hall, and I was on my way to the locker room right before I was stopped. George Saffold was tall, a little rough around the edges, and he wore his hair in long cornrows. He was a little different from the guys I was usually attracted to, so I was a bit surprised when he walked up to me. With it only being months after Chandi's death, I still wasn't quite ready to socialize with anyone.

"Hey, I noticed you changed your hair," he said.

I smiled at his weak attempt to make conversation. For months, I noticed George checking me out, but his timing was way off now.

"Yeah, I did," I replied dryly. Surprisingly, my nonchalant attitude didn't deter him in the least. George studied me in silence. It made me a little nervous, and the hairs on the back of my neck instantly stood up.

"Hey, why don't you talk no more?" he finally asked.

I didn't respond immediately. Instead, I mulled over his question. There were a number of reasons, but I chose the most obvious. "I recently lost a friend," I answered in a low tone, "I haven't been feeling like myself since."

"Chandi McMillan?"

I nodded my head in silence. George walked up to me and placed his hand on my small shoulder. His touch was comforting instead of flirtatious. Staring deeply in my eyes, he said, "You can't be walking around blaming yourself, baby girl. Some things in life are bigger than us."

A slight smile tugged at my lips. It was the first time in weeks. George's wise words of compassion cheered me up almost instantaneously, and I was suddenly looking at him in a completely new light. A few days later in the gymnasium, I gave an emotional speech about strength and unity. It had taken me weeks to write the compelling words, and even longer to get the courage to read them in front of the school. In the midst of my crucial sermon, one of the jocks rudely yelled out, "Shut up with your Skittle-head looking ass!"

Immediately, the entire gymnasium erupted in laughter. My cheeks flushed in embarrassment, but I tried my best not to get discouraged. Swallowing my pride, I continued my speech until I was finally met with a well-deserved applause. Not even an insult could deter my mission. That night, however, I mulled over the joke tossed at me. Little did he know he had given me the perfect name to compliment my unique personality.

***

"I started to get up and drill him over that corny line. He had no right even disrespecting you like that." George told me on the phone that night. He wasn't all too pleased with the insult I had gotten during my speech. I even had to stop him from confronting the guy outside of the gymnasium after it was over.

I smiled into the receiver and twirled a pink curly strand of hair around my finger. "This might actually sound surprising, but I think I might like the name Skittlez."

Over the next few weeks, I found myself hanging out with George more and more. Every night we would talk on the phone until we fell asleep in mid-sentence. In a world where few loved me and no one understood me, it was nice to have someone in my corner for a change. Eventually, I began to feel like my old self again. With George as my self-proclaimed support system, it felt good to come back to reality. He had me acting like the old Mary while selflessly helping me to heal from my loss. Since I was fourteen and George was sixteen, the school was in an uproar when they found out we were dating. He was a popular junior on the basketball team, and to them I was just an average freshman. I didn't mind it at all, because a lot of girls liked George, but I knew it came along with the territory. George had a part-time job as a dishwasher at a nearby diner. He also owned a car, so money, and transportation were never an issue. Every Friday night, we went to a popular skating rink to hang out with our friends from school. Whether George knew it or not, he really helped me come out of my shell again. My life finally felt like the clouds were disappearing. George was my sun, and he made me more than happy.

During my break from the world, I took up another hobby. I began to design my own clothing by taking pictures, using transparency and ironing them on t-shirts. Afterwards, I would cut around the top and sew it onto my jeans, so that it resembled a collage. My goal was to ensure that my attire was unlike any other current brand out. The craft was rather tedious, but I loved it. George was all for my newfound interest. Diane, on the other hand, thought it was a waste of time and good clothing. She also wasn't too thrilled with my new boyfriend. Many times, we had arguments that resulted in me defending George's case. She felt like he was too old for me, and she didn't trust his intentions. Still, her opinions didn't stop me from hanging out with him.

All was well until one Friday evening when I was preparing to leave with George for the skating rink. He'd called me to let me know that he was on his way. As usual, I made sure that I was dressed, but the moment I came downstairs, I was met with an unpleasant stare from my mother. Judging from her expression, I could tell that something was bothering her.

"Where are you going?" she asked grimly.

Moving around her, I headed towards the front door. Normally, I waited for George to pick me up on the porch. "To the skating rink, Ma," I answered nonchalantly, "I go every week. You know that."

Diane frowned at my careless attitude. "I know that?" she repeated, "No, what I know is you been getting' a lil' too comfortable with that boy." She propped her closed fists on her narrow hips. "I heard he was in a gang."

"Ma," I whined. "He's not in a gang. He's the star of the basketball team. What are you talking about?" I hated that I was even entertaining the conversation with her. Now that I had someone, who made me happy, my mother was trying to tear him away. It was if she didn't want me to dependent upon anyone but her.

"You're not going anywhere tonight," Diane said with finality, "So you may as well just march yourself upstairs and change."

"Ma…"

"Now," she barked, "And I won't repeat myself."

In a fit of rage, I raced upstairs to my bedroom and slammed the door. Tears filled my eyes as I flopped onto my flimsy twin size bed. Fed up with my mother and her ridiculous beliefs, I snatched out my cellphone and called the only person I could think of. An hour later, I was in the passenger seat of Avon's baby mother's Toyota. Candace and my older brother had been dating on-and-off for several years, and she was the closest thing to a big sister I had. She always lent an ear whenever I needed someone to talk to, and she understood my teenage dilemmas and me. She'd even gone out of her way to make a forty-five minute drive just to pick me up. On the way back to her house, I filled her in on everything from my new love to my mother's sudden change of heart. George and I had been dating for months, and she picked that day to finally speak up on it. I didn't understand her logic, and I felt as if she were purposely giving me a hard time because she was bitter and lonely, and she wanted me to be lonely too.

"I'm sure she's only trying to protect you," Candace said in a concerned tone, "I mean I know how it is. I was your age once. I know what it's like to have your first boyfriend. You want independence. But believe me when I say it, Mary, my only regret in life is growing up too fast."

As Candace spoke words of wisdom to me, I stared out of the passenger window. It wasn't even sunset yet, and the skies were unusually gloomy. Ironically, they matched my mood. When we finally made it to her house, I talked to Candace until I fell asleep.

Suddenly, I was yanked out the bed in the middle of the night.

"Mary, wake up," Candace yelled frantically, "You have to get up! You need to watch the news."

Groaning softly, I wiped the sleep from my eyes and sat up in bed. "What is it?"

"Come into the living room. Quick!" Candace grabbed me by wrist, and I half-walked half-ran into the living room. On her thirty-two inch television, was a news story.

"What did you say George's last name was?" Candace quickly asked.

"Saffold," I replied. My expression was one of pure confusion.

Candace hastily ran over to the TV and turned up the volume.

"Developing news on a story where one teenage boy lost his life tonight in a deadly shootout. Sixteen-year old George Saffold was inside of his parked vehicle at the local Roll and Skate when..."

The news reporter's voice trailed off as my mind went blank. Suddenly, my vision blurred. A strong sensation of lightheadedness took over me, and I had to sit on the nearby sofa to keep from collapsing.

"I am so sorry," Candace whispered.

There wasn't a single light on in the room. The lights from the television danced against her smooth dark brown skin. From where I sat, I could see the tears forming in her eyes.

My voice cracked when I finally spoke. "This can't be happening again…"

Mz. Skittlez

***

Not even three months after Chandi's death and I'd already lost another close friend just weeks shy of my fifteenth birthday. Only this person was my first kiss and the love of my young life. I'd worked so hard on building myself up again after Chandi's untimely passing only for George to die too. It just wasn't fair. I didn't understand God's message at all. Why was he punishing me? Over the next few days, I slowly began to lose myself. Reverting back to my old ways, I wrote suicide letters to my father again. In an effort to uplift and encourage me, he sent me gifts from prison. I could've cared less about those. I needed a way out and my father was now my only escape. Someway and somehow, I mustered up enough courage to get up and go to school every day. Most times, I was late and wound up sent to the principal's office. One morning in particular, I encountered a fellow female student in the office. Because we were both waiting to be seen by the principal, it only seemed natural to speak. Besides, I hadn't spoken to anyone since George's funeral. I had to keep my distance from the other students.

"What are you in here for?" I asked as if we were roommates in a holding cell.

"I just found out I'm pregnant," she revealed with a somber expression.

My mouth dropped open in surprise because she looked no older than I was. With wide doe eyes, soft and innocent features, it was clearly obvious that she was still a baby herself.

"Really?"

The young girl nodded her head. "I'm leaving school to talk to my boyfriend's mother," she said, "He doesn't want me to, but I have to tell someone. My parents aren't around, and I really don't know what else to do."

I opened my mouth to respond but was caught off guard when Principal Jenkins called out my name. Before I got up, I wished the girl luck. I couldn't imagine what she was going through.

Later that night, I discovered that her boyfriend had killed her. He shot her in the garage of his home in a brutal fit of rage. Immediately, I felt as if I had been cursed. Everyone I ran into seemed to drop like flies. After that incident, I completely withdrew from everyone. I dreaded the thought of getting close to people for fear that I'd lose them as well. I refused to date anyone else, and making friends was totally out of the question. I gradually became a hollow shell of myself. Fed up with life and the tragedies that plagued mine, I wrote my father a final letter. In the note, I explained that would be the last time he would hear from me if he didn't come to get me after he got out. That summer I finally got my wish.

***

A few months after my father's release, he came to Indianapolis and took me back to Ohio with him. He was a bit more financially stable than Diane was, and was able to offer a much better environment for me. On the long drive back to Cleveland, we talked and tried our best to make up for lost time. It was tough considering all the turmoil I had gone through over the years. I could tell from the way he tensed up at the mention of my mother's name that he loathed her and all that she had put me through.

When we finally touched down, it felt like I'd entered a completely new world. It had been years since I lived there. I couldn't recall what the city looked like before, but I knew that it was the complete opposite of Indianapolis. Although I knew it would take some adjusting, I was more than ready for the challenge. Besides, being anywhere new felt like a breath of fresh air.

My eyes instantly grew wide when we finally pulled into the driveway of a huge red house. "Is this your house?" I asked in amazement.

Art chuckled and shifted the gears into park. "Not quite," he answered, "My cousin Rudy and her husband Parker do. There's more than enough room for you here," he quickly added.

My head swiveled in his direction with a look of disappointment lining my face. "So I won't be living with you?" I asked trying to mask my irritation.

"You told me to save you," Art said, "and that's what I'm doing, baby girl." His expression was humorless as he stared deeply into my eyes.

Taking a deep breath, I swallowed my pride and opened the passenger door. Art followed suit before grabbing my belongings. Together we walked side-by-side to the large red house. Initially, I wasn't too keen with the idea of living with Rudy, but when I thought about it, anywhere was better than living in Indianapolis with Diane. I figured my father didn't want me to live with him because of his new girlfriend. Perhaps he felt as if he'd be inconveniencing her with my presence. Either way, beggars couldn't be choosers.

5

"Fly with me…or watch me from the ground."

    I quickly found out that living with Rudy wasn't as dreadful as I thought it would be. As a matter of fact, she actually felt like a savior by taking me in without expecting anything in return. Over time, she became like a second mother to me, instilling in me the wisdom I needed to successfully navigate through my teenage years. She kept me on track and generally grounded me in life. Diane and my relationship eventually became distant, and we rarely if ever spoke. But then again that was the norm when it came to us. Even while living together we rarely communicated. In all honesty, I really wanted to stay as far away from her as possible. I didn't need her negative energy now that my life was finally going accordingly. Adjusting to Cleveland again was just as hard as I thought it would be. However, it felt good to start over. All I wanted to do now was put all of the pain and death behind me. Rudy and her husband encouraged me to do better. Upon moving in with her, she got me back in pageants and music. Rudy motivated me to be the best I could be. She cared and supported my endeavors as if I were her own child. They made me believe in life and family again. And I also idolized Parker as a man, and swore to myself that one day I would marry a guy just like him. I loved the romance between him and his wife and wished for the same one day. Any time I needed fatherly advice or got frustrated with life in general, Parker eagerly stepped up and took on the role of my godfather. Rudy and Parker were my only support system at the time since my father was too busy with his girlfriend and career.

    Art McCoy had devoted his entire livelihood to becoming a civil rights activist. The city referred to him as the "Modern day MLK." He did everything from protesting to searching for missing people. Everyone knew him, and everyone respected him because of what he did. Although I was proud of my father, I really wished that he could've been a part of my life more especially when he'd missed out on so much already, but he was a working man whose career came before anything else. Art also owned a barbershop downtown, and several small businesses in the East Cleveland area. He was an entrepreneur, and simply didn't have the time to raise a teenage daughter. Instead of giving me the time I longed for, my father bought my love with material things. Paying for my attention, he went over and beyond to spoil me by any means to make up for what he lacked. On my sixteenth birthday, he bought me a car making my teenage dream come true. My father and I didn't have the ideal relationship I craved, but it was good enough.

At Shaw High School, everyone wanted to be my friend because of the things I owned and who my father was. And since I wanted to fit in, I dealt with the fake friendships. The worst part of it all was starting over again. Back home everyone knew who I was, the colorfully eccentric girl with the under-bite. My flaws were no longer a joke. Shaw was definitely a step down from the performing arts academy I was once enrolled in. Determined to find my niche in school, I began playwriting. During the first semester of the year, I became involved with the NAACP. Later on, I created a powerful play called "Tragedy High." The script was loosely based on my experiences at Broadripple, and mainly focused on how to prevent suicide. The play offered a beautiful and positive message, and I'd even won an award for my creation.

Along the way, I befriended a girl named Cashua who was three years older than I was. We had met at a local talent show and clicked instantly. Her love for music was just as strong as mine, and she had big dreams of one day becoming a rapper. She was 5'4", brown-skinned, and had shoulder length hair. She'd had a son with her previous boyfriend but was left alone to fend for her child herself. Sometime after meeting her, Cashua began dating Rudy's son Darcel. Unfortunately, they didn't last very long, but still she ended up getting pregnant unexpectedly. Darcel and Cash fought constantly about the decision of whether or not she should keep the baby. Since he already had children, Darcel was completely against claiming anymore. He wanted Cash to get an abortion and had no problem letting her know. Countless nights, I sat on the phone listening to my girl curse out Darcel and every other useless man that had ever hurt her.

With limited options available, Cashua began dancing full-time at Magic City on St Clair. She used the fact that she wasn't showing yet to her advantage. Soon our hangouts became far and few in between. By the time she had gotten big, we completely lost touch. It wasn't until after her daughter Chardae was born that she finally came back around. Cash eagerly appointed me as godmother since I was the only real friend she had. I was the one who gave her only daughter the nickname Apples. Cash and I hung out a few times after that, but just as quickly as we rekindled again, our relationship became distant. A few months after giving birth to Apples, Cash started stripping again and fell in with the wrong crowd. She also picked up a few nasty habits like drinking excessively and doing drugs. Soon, one thing led to another and she received a visit from Child Protective Services. Apples was only a year-old when she and her brother were taken from Cash's custody. Since Cash had no one else to help her out in her time of turmoil, I bravely stepped up to the plate. At the tender age of sixteen, I adopted Apples. Other than the fact that Cash was my friend, I simply didn't want to see her wind up in foster care. Because I had no prior experience with raising babies, I was forced to take parenting classes. Although, it was a lot to deal with still being in high school, I did it for Cash. I also figured that Rudy and Parker took me in, so why not take Apples in too? Unfortunately, Darcel didn't come around much because of his strained relationship with his parents. You would've thought he'd be mature enough to put his differences aside, but sadly, that wasn't the case.

 I really didn't mind taking care of Apples at all; however, the responsibility placed upon me did force me to grow up fast. I now had someone to look after. I treated Apples as if she was my sibling, being her mother was not what I was aiming for. I wanted her to grow up and look at me as a big sister. And in all actuality, having her around grew on me pretty quickly. Born with somewhat of a maternal instinct, taking care of Apples came to me naturally, but what I wasn't expecting was for Cash to become jealous of me shortly after. Apparently, she was angry at the fact that I had taken in Apples and not her son. Eventually, she'd stopped talking to me altogether out of spite feeling as though I was taking away her only daughter. The love and respect Cash had for me slowly turned into hate. On several occasions, I tried my best to reason with her, and each time she didn't want to hear it. In her eyes, I was the big, bad wolf who came knocking on her door to take her child away. On social media sites, Cash even went as far as to trash my name and me. She did everything she possibly could to get under my skin, but I tried my best not to entertain her childishness. A few months shy of Apples' third birthday, I enrolled her in a baby beauty pageant and invited Cash to come. I would've never expected for her to bring her drama with her. She had embarrassed me throughout the entire event that I had no choice but to check her in the parking lot afterward.

"What is up with you? You've been giving me a hard time since this whole ordeal, and all I've ever done was try to help you."

Cash was almost to her car when I caught up with her. Apples, of course, was right by my side. I could tell from Cash's expression that the sight of it all bothered her tremendously, yet what could I do when I was only doing what she asked me to do?

"You didn't help me," she spat, "You helped yourself!" With that said, she jumped in her car, slammed the door, and sped off. She didn't bother telling her own daughter goodbye.

Even though I was now raising a child full-time, Rudy and Parker made sure I was as active in school as possible. They felt that if I kept my head in my books, I wouldn't be distracted with what was going on around me. Living in Cleveland, it was so easy for a teenager to fall victim to the street life. And it was even easier for a girl my age to get distracted by guys with hidden motives. For most of the school year, I did well avoiding both until the afternoon I met Deyontay Binds.

***

Deyontay was the total opposite of what I usually went for. Dark-skinned, slender, and a bit rough around the edges, I would've never given him a second look had he not approached me. The day I'd met Deyontay, I was walking down the school steps when I suddenly dropped my books. Very much the gentleman, he quickly rushed to my aid and picked up my items.

"Thank you so much," I told him, "I really appreciate it. I can be so clumsy sometimes."

"No problem at all, ma," he said handing me my Algebra and English textbook.

Our fingers brushed gently against each other's during the encounter. Jolts of electricity shot throughout my body, and I couldn't

The Icing On Top Ain't Always Sweet

explain the feeling in the pit of my stomach. For a second, I assumed they were butterflies, but that couldn't be right because I wasn't the least bit attracted to him.

"I'll see you around," he smiled before walking off.

A few days later, Deyontay began passing notes to me in school. At that time, it was the most popular form of communicating. In the beginning, I didn't reply immediately. As a matter of fact, I made him sweat for a few weeks before finally giving him the time of day. Truth be told, Deyontay was far from being my type. He had no swag, and his clothes were always worn and oversized almost as if they were hand me downs. I was embarrassed to be seen with a guy like him. He was a freshman, and I was a popular sophomore on the cheerleading team. Nevertheless, he was a sweetheart and went out his way to prove himself to me. Deyontay did the little things that spoke volumes like bringing me lunch from his job. He also treated me like gold, placing me on a pedestal that was well above his own. Pleased with his overwhelming effort, I finally decided to give Deyontay a real chance. But first thing was first. He needed a makeover and bad. Within weeks of dating, I quickly got Deyontay's style together. The very first day we made it official, I left school and returned with a brand new pack of white t-shirts. I refused to be seen with Deyontay and his baggy jeans and holey shirts. And after getting his wardrobe together, I didn't mind being seen with him. The outside finally matched the inside.

Deyontay and I communicated on a daily basis by texting and passing notes. Two months barely elapsed and already we had fallen for each other. He had me gone, and I'd never been as strongly attracted to someone as I was to him. Deyontay said the smoothest things and treated me like I was the only girl he saw.

The very first day Deyontay brought me to his home, he was embarrassed. Before we even went inside, he warned me that they didn't have much.

"It isn't fancy, so don't be expecting the Ritz."

I laughed and shook my head at his obvious insecurities. Honestly, that was the least of my concern. One of the things I liked most about him was the fact that we both had troubled pasts. I had once been homeless, and as a child, Deyontay's only means of shelter was a rickety, old attic.

"Boy, you are so silly. I'm not," I told him, "Now stop tripping, and let's go inside."

Hesitantly, Deyontay shut off the ignition and opened his door. After climbing out his Monte Carlo, he walked around the car and opened the passenger door for me. Since the neighborhood wasn't the best my expectations weren't high about what the inside of his house looked like. But then again, I really didn't care. I was simply happy that he'd extended the invitation. At sixteen, he was the first boy that had ever invited me over. Taking my hand in his, Deyontay led me towards his home. That very night I became a woman. After losing my virginity, I was deeply in love with Deyontay. He became my entire life, and my love for him was so strong that it clouded my otherwise good sense of judgment. Suddenly, having a baby by him seemed more important than finishing high school. Eventually, it even became a priority. Every night and day, Deyontay and I talked about conceiving. It seemed like the perfect idea, and since I took exceptional care of Apples, I knew that I would be a great mom. It didn't matter that I had a bright future ahead of me. I was willing to let it all go for Deyontay, the music, the cheerleading, the designing, everything. Love had a way of making a person crazy. Growing up Diane had always preached that a female's womanhood was like a tree. "Every time you have premarital sex, you lose a leaf," she would often say. But at that point, I was too gone over Deyontay to even care.

***

Two Years Later…

Deyontay quickly gained a rep as being the bad boy every girl dreamt about, and he fought with any guy who tried to tell him otherwise. Since I upgraded his appearance, he had gotten big headed. Soon his reputation had caused him to be expelled. He was only in the eleventh grade when Shaw finally kicked him out. Although I didn't want to admit it, I had created a monster. Deyontay had gotten so full of himself that he carelessly flirted with girls as if I didn't exist anymore. He even had the nerve to get upset if I confronted him about it. Deyontay felt he deserved to be able to flirt with any female he wanted while still keeping me. He was out of control, and there wasn't a single person able to tame him. Yet regardless of his obvious flaws, I was more than willing to make it work with him. I loved Deyontay just that much.

During spring break of my junior year, I got my first pregnancy scare. While at my first period class, I became so nauseous that I needed to excuse myself. Instead of heading to the bathroom, I ditched school and drove to the nearest Dollar General. I felt like I was walking the green mile as I slowly walked down the aisle leading to the First Response pregnancy tests.

What are my godparents going to think of me? I asked myself. *How's Deyontay going to react if I wind up pregnant? Will he leave me? Will he stay? Would we be able to make it work?*

A dozen questions flooded my mind as I reached for one of the tests. My heart thumped wildly in my chest as I headed towards the counter. I was supposed to be in school, and yet I was in a dollar store preparing to buy a pregnancy test. When I finally reached the counter, I noticed the cashier eyeing me suspiciously. Even without her saying anything, I could tell what she was thinking.

"Will this be all?" she asked scanning the barcode.

"Yes," I mumbled. My voice came out cracked. I was overwhelmed with emotion.

After purchasing the test, I rushed out the store and headed straight to Deyontay's house.

Two positive pregnancy tests confirmed what I already knew in the back of my mind. Of course, I never told anyone other than Deyontay for fear of what they'd think or say. Surprisingly, he wasn't upset by the news. If anything, he was thrilled by the fact that he was going to be a father. He had even gone as far as to demand that I stop cheerleading. He claimed that he didn't want me to overexert myself and miscarry. I continued to do it anyway, but behind his back. Cheerleading was the only thing that made me feel like a normal teen considering that I was now thrown into the new world of motherhood. Over the next few weeks, my body slowly underwent changes. I was always tired and certain smells were intolerable. Every day when Deyontay got off work, I made him take his clothes off before greeting me since the smell made me nauseous. It wasn't long before word got out around the school that Deyontay and I were expecting a baby. I was barely two months by then. The only person who didn't know was my godmother, Rudy. The only reason I chose to keep my pregnancy from her was because I knew she would be disappointed. Rudy and Parker had gone over and beyond to ensure that something like that wouldn't happen, and I had let them down. Feeling as though I had to step up and take responsibility for my actions, I approached Rudy one evening about getting a job.

"A job? What do you need a job for?" she asked moving around the seared chicken she was cooking in the skillet. Even while working full-time and taking care of our grandfather who lived there as well, Rudy always made sure to provide a home cooked meal every night.

Nervously, I shuffled from one foot to the other. "I need money to support myself and my family...," I simply said.

Rudy gave a lighthearted laugh, but immediately stopped after realizing how serious I truly was. "Are you having sex?" she asked with a straight face.

All of the color immediately flushed from my face. I could feel myself tense up as Rudy stared at me. "I—uh..."

Grabbing my upper arm, Rudy shook me lightly. "Answer me!"

"No," I lied.

"Tell the truth! You're having sex, aren't you?"

Spit splattered onto my face as Rudy continued to yell. Tears filled her almond-shaped eyes as disappointment and hurt was on her face.

"Let me go!" I said trying to snatch my arm away. Rudy's vice grip on my arm was intolerable.

"You're not my mother. I don't need you!"

Rudy propped her hands on her wide hips. "Well, if you don't need me then you can get out!"

Rebelliously, I agreed. "I will. As a matter of fact, I'm gonna live with my dad."

Before Rudy could reply, I ran upstairs and packed up my belongings. Seventeen, pregnant, and in love, I thought I had it all figured out. Little did I know how wrong I really was.

6

"Trust takes years to build, seconds to break and a lifetime to repair..."

I moved in with my father immediately after being kicked out of Rudy's home. Ironically, he lived right across the street with his new girlfriend. My dad pretty much allowed me to do whatever I pleased in order to make up for the fact that he often neglected me. That and also because he was always out handling business. Deyontay and I carried ourselves as if we were adults instead of teenagers. Since we were under the impression that we were going to be new parents, we acted as such. My father didn't put up a fight at all even though he knew what was going on. I was rarely home, and I spent most nights at Deyontay's. I was there so much; it was like I lived there. Although Rudy and I didn't speak much after our whole ordeal, I still visited frequently to take care of Apples. Regardless of what was going on, she was still a priority in my life. As the weeks went by Deyontay's head grew bigger and bigger. So much so that I thought, it was going to swell from arrogance. He was finally letting the hype get to him, and I was fed up. He barely had a chance to get in the house that afternoon before I berated him with questions.

"Where were you? You got off work three hours ago."

"Skittlez, don't come at me with that. Besides, why you keeping up with my schedule anyway?"

"For scenarios like this."

Deyontay walked around me and headed towards his bedroom. He didn't even speak to his little brother Jarrod who sat at the dining room table doing his homework.

"Just be real. You're messing around!" I yelled following after him.

Deyontay stopped in mid-step nearly causing me to collide with his back. In a fit of rage, he whirled around to face me. "I'm sick of you with this insecure crap. If you don't trust me, why are you even here? Go home!"

Stunned by his reaction, I stood with my mouth wide open. "Fine! I'm outta here. Do whatever you want. I know I am!" With that said, I grabbed my purse and stormed out of the front door.

It had only been three weeks since mine and Deyontay's break up. I was nearing four months by then, and even though I despised his new cocky attitude, I really missed him. The last thing I wanted was to go through the pregnancy alone. Every day at school was torture. Word spread around school that we had broken up, and Deyontay didn't make it any better. Every afternoon right after school let out, he pulled up to the parking lot playing his music as he could. He wasn't even enrolled in school anymore, so I he was only there just to annoy me. One day in particular I caught him talking to Stephanie Banks, a well-known girl from the volleyball team. Their flirtatious interaction caught me off-guard since she used to refer to him as a play brother, but anytime I suspected something between them, Deyontay would always reassure me by telling me that they were just friends. I'd even gone as far as to confront Stephanie, but she claimed the same that they were only really good friends. Jealousy surged through my body, but I tried my best to hide it as I headed to my car.

"Deyontay, say bye to your baby mama," she teased.

Ignoring Stephanie and my ex-boyfriend, I climbed inside my vehicle and skirted off. Surprisingly, that night I received a phone call from Deyontay pleading for me to take him back. Although I tried to play hard to get by making him grovel, I was relieved that he had come to his senses. It was comforting to know that he missed me as much as I missed him. Determined to make up for lost time, Deyontay invited me over his house after school. But like the saying goes, *people never change*. An hour after talking to him on the phone, he called back and told me not to come because he was leaving out for the night. Baffled and disappointed by his sudden change in heart, I hesitantly agreed. Shortly after, I received a call from his little brother Jarrod. "Hey, J, what's up?" I asked in a cracked tone trying my best to mask my sadness.

"Sis, Dee's gotta girl over here," the twelve-year old blurted out.

My eyes widened in shock and disbelief. I immediately sat up in my bed and stared straight ahead. I couldn't believe my ears. I knew

The Icing On Top Ain't Always Sweet

right away that he wasn't lying because we had a bond that was stronger than his and Deyontay's. Unlike his older brother who often neglected him, I paid ample attention to Jarrod and even helped with his homework when I could. Since their mom was too doped up on medications to cook and properly care for him, I took on the role of doing her chores. Because of my effort, Jarrod loved and respected me like I was his own flesh and blood.

"Come, sis. Come!" he yelled frantically.

Quickly disconnecting the call, I hopped out of bed and ran downstairs. Upon stepping outside, I suddenly remembered that my car was having problems. However, I was on a mission. Wearing four-inch heels, I started towards Deyontay's home which was located only a couple blocks from my own. Nothing was more dangerous than a woman scorned especially an angry, pregnant woman scorned. Halfway to my destination, I stopped at my friend Charmaine's home. There I filled her in on everything before changing into a spare pair of her tennis shoes. They were a size too small, but I was too determined to care. After thanking her, I rushed out and continued my journey. I was only a block or two away when my play brother William pulled alongside me in his gunmetal colored Cadillac. Much like myself, he was heavily involved in the world of music. He was also a part of a local rap group known as The Taliban.

"You need a ride?" he yelled out the passenger window.

Without a word, I climbed inside and fastened my seat belt. William could tell from the stressed look on my face that something was bothering me.

"Aye, you good, ma?"

"I will be soon," I told him, "I need you to take me to Deyontay's house."

William switched gears and pulled off, "Say no more."

Five minutes later, we pulled alongside Deyontay's rundown home. As expected, his car was parked directly in the driveway.

"You need me to come in with you?" William asked interrupting my thoughts.

"No, I think I got it," I told him.

"I mean, if he puts his hands on you, I'm coming in," he added.

I smiled weakly before climbing out, "Thank you."

My heart thumped rapidly in my chest as I walked towards the front door. On the way there, I didn't have a clue on what I'd say to Deyontay upon seeing him. Jarrod anxiously swung the front door open before I could even lift my hand to twist the knob. "He's in the basement," he told me with wide, alert eyes.

Heading towards the door that led to the basement, I took a deep breath before I opened it. My heart was beating so hard that I thought it might explode out of my chest. I started wheezing due to my asthma, and I suddenly remembered that I left my inhaler at home, but that was the last thing on my mind as I opened the door and descended the stairs.

"Deyontay?" I called out.

No response.

When I finally got to the foot of the stairs, my mouth instantly fell open. The television in front of the bed was on, and on the bed sat Deyontay and Stephanie Banks.

"You liar. I hate you!" I screamed.

In a fit of rage, I picked up Deyontay's nearby sneakers and threw them at him. He immediately shielded himself from the blow.

"Skittlez, chill!" he yelled. He looked so pathetic that I couldn't believe I had once loved him.

"I can't believe you," I yelled shoving him away, "You told me not to come, so you could do this?"

"Skittlez, I…"

WHAP!

Deyontay's sentence was immediately cut short after my hand met his cheek.

"I'ma let you have that one," he said holding the side of his face, "At least let me walk her to the bus stop, so we can talk like we got some sense."

"You're not walking her anywhere!"

"Get out my way." Deyontay made a move to walk around me, but I raced to the stairs and blocked his path. Each time he tried to walk past me, I pushed him back down. I refused to allow him to walk her home.

"This is childish," she said, "I'm leaving." Fed up with our antics, she hastily put on her shoes on. Once she was done, she started to walk up the stairs past me. Without warning, I sent a devastating kick to her midsection that sent her flying backwards. Stephanie landed on the concrete floor with a hard thud. The look of fear in her eyes was unavoidable.

"What is wrong with you, girl?" Deyontay barked. He manhandled me with such force as he grabbed and tossed me onto his bed. It was still damp from their bodies' sweat.

Deyontay then rushed to Stephanie's aid and helped her up. It was as if I'd meant nothing to him. A couple months ago, we were out shopping for baby clothes, and now we were fighting like cats and dogs. Going against my demands, Deyontay walked Stephanie to the bus stop leaving me all alone. Set on making him feel exactly how I did, I snatched up all his precious belongings and put them in a sheet. Afterwards, I called up Charmaine and told her to pick me up. I figured William had pulled off assuming Deyontay and I had reconciled. When my friend and her sister finally arrived, I placed the bundled up sheet inside their trunk. Deyontay walked up just as I was preparing to climb into the car. He wore a look of irritation on his face like he was the one who'd been cheated on.

"Where's my phone? I know you have it."

"I don't know what you're talking…" Before I could finish, Deyontay snatched my purse and ran off. I quickly jumped into my girls' car, and we proceeded to follow him to the end of the street. Judging from his body language, I could tell that he was tired of playing, so I got out and approached him.

"Give me my phone, and I'll give you your stuff."

Defeated, I pulled out his cellphone and started to hand it over. Out of nowhere, an idea came to mind. Right in front of Deyontay, I unlocked his home screen and went directly to the messages.

"What are you doing?" he asked with an apprehensive expression.

Ignoring him, I scrolled through Stephanie's messages. They'd been flirting for weeks, and some of the dates were even when Deyontay and I were still together.

"Give me my phone." Deyontay quickly ran up and snatched it out my hand, and instead of handing me my purse, he childishly tossed it at my feet.

"You deserve whatever that nasty girl gives you," I laughed, "You lost a good one." With that said, I grabbed his stuff out the trunk and threw it into the busy street. Items of clothing flew everywhere, and I immediately felt a sense of relief.

Deyontay dropped down onto his knees and stared at the horrific scene before him. All of his nice clothes were now ruined just like the trust I once had for him. Climbing back into the car, my girls and I rode off listening to Kelly Rowland's "Here We Go Again."

***

Only hours after my spat with Deyontay, I went straight to the school's basketball game to cheer. My friends tried their best to build me up and help me forget about him, but Deyontay made it impossible. Every day after school, he would show up to talk to other girls just to spite me. When it was obvious that I wouldn't budge, he finally caved once again.

"We need to talk," he told me over the phone one evening. "We need to get our lives together. If not for our sake, for our child's. We're about to have a baby."

That was all I needed to hear before I was once again his. Even with everything Deyontay had taken me through, I loved him unconditionally. He was my first real love, and I wasn't ready to let it go just yet. We had to fight for the sake of our unborn child.

***

Deyontay and I were in Tower City shopping for infant's clothes when I felt a sharp pain rip through my tummy. "I—I have to go to the bathroom," I told him before rushing off.

We were standing in line at Subway in the food court when the agony hit me. Luckily, the public restroom wasn't too far. As soon as I made it inside an empty stall, I fell down onto the toilet seat. Almost instantly, blood gushed out. Panic shook my senses, as I feared the worse. The pain in my stomach was intolerable. Unfortunately, I had no pads, my phone was dead, and I was the only person in the restroom.

"Help!" I screamed in hopes that someone nearby would hear me, "Somebody, please help me!"

No one rushed to my rescue, and I was forced to sit on the toilet in agony and discomfort. I didn't understand what was going on. I had never been so afraid in my entire life.

After ten or fifteen minutes of waiting, Deyontay finally came and yelled out my name. "Skittlez, what's taking you so long in there? Yo, you straight?"

"Deyontay? Is that you? Please come in here and help me!"

He quickly rushed inside the restroom, once he heard the panic in my voice. He opened the stall's door and stared down at me in confusion. "What the hell is going on?"

"Oh, my God! It hurts so much. Please help me!" I cried.

"I think you're miscarrying."

"No, no, no! Don't say that," I sobbed uncontrollably.

Deyontay carefully lifted me off the toilet and carried me to the train. There he called my father and informed him of what was happening. By then I was losing consciousness and blood incredibly fast. I was barely alert by the time I arrived at the hospital. After I was given oxygen and promptly treated, I was informed by a nurse that I was never pregnant. Apparently, my body had undergone a drastic change that resulted in a temporary absence of my cycle. The change was brought about from overexertion from cheerleading. I was so ashamed and embarrassed by what I'd found out that I didn't want to tell a soul.

No, I told myself, *I can't let him find out.*

Deyontay and I had just rekindled, and I didn't want to lose him again. Although it was wrong, I went ahead and allowed him and everyone else to believe that I was pregnant and had miscarried. When Deyontay finally came into the delivery room, I was silent with a blank stare on my face. He, of course, thought it was because of our tragic loss. He had no idea that I was disturbed by the fact that I was never pregnant. We had gone out and purchased baby clothes, but now what were we going to do? What were we going to say to people who asked? Taking one look at the pink and blue blankets in the room, he asked, "We were having twins after all, huh?"

All of a sudden, I broke out into tears. Deyontay quickly rushed to my side and held me close. "It's gonna be okay," he promised, "Everything's gonna be straight. You got me, and I got you, baby girl, and because of that we can get through anything together."

***

Deyontay was determined to make another baby after the so-called miscarriage. What he didn't know was that I'd secretly gotten on birth control to avoid getting pregnant. That scare was enough to last me a lifetime. I loved Deyontay with all my heart and soul, but I was also terrified of losing him. Eventually, he got tired of my neediness, which ultimately caused a strain in our relationship. I'd become so dependent upon him that I almost had a nervous breakdown after he mentioned that we needed to take some time apart. I wasn't with it, but then again, I didn't have a choice. At one point, I stopped going to school completely to avoid seeing Deyontay, but seemingly, I couldn't live without him. I called him up some time later asking if he could visit me since I didn't feel good. As expected, he rudely shot me down.

"Man, no. Besides, I know you playing games." Deyontay's tone was laced with irritation. I could clearly tell that he was sick of my antics.

CLICK!

He hung up before I could even respond. Feeling as though I had a point to prove, I dialed up the ambulance even though I wasn't the least bit ill. My whole purpose was to find out if he still loved me. I figured if he came then obviously, he cared, but if he didn't then I had to let it go. The fact that Deyontay didn't show up afterwards was really the eye-opener I desperately needed. I had called several times and left a few text messages explaining that I was on my way to the hospital. Surprisingly, he didn't bother calling me back to make sure that I was okay. As much as I didn't want to believe and accept that I'd actually lost him, it was finally time for me to move on whether I wanted to or not.

In the midst of everything I'd gone through, I managed to keep a close relationship with Apples who was still living with Rudy. Now that Deyontay was out of my life, I could focus on what was most important like school and my passion for music and fashion. I now had to focus on myself while setting a good example for my goddaughter. Like they say, *all good things must come to an end.* I knew that it was over. In the midst of everything I'd gone through with Deyontay, I was finally able to focus on what was important in my life, like school, my passion for music, and fashion. With my head back on my shoulders, I got into beauty pageants again. It was the one thing Diane had introduced me to that I'd stuck with. I loved competing and being on stage is where I shined the most. For a moment, I was able to forget who I was and be who I wanted to be.

7
"Life's under no obligation to give us what we expect…"

After school, I usually came home to practice my routines. Practice makes perfect, so that's what I did. Deciding on a contemporary dance piece for the talent portion of the pageant, I hurried across the street to show Rudy what I had been working so hard on. Once Deyontay and I broke up, Rudy was the only person who I could confide in. She had been there so much for me in the past that I became lost without her motherly guidance. She apologized for her overreaction when I told her that I was pregnant.

"I just want the best for you. That's all. I see that light in you, girl, and I want you to let it shine."

It felt good to know that I had someone in my corner. After being transplanted from one place to the other, with Rudy, Parker, and Apples, I felt at home. As I walked into the house, I yelled out for Rudy with excitement. She was a tough critique, but there was no way she could find fault with this dance. I had been working on it for weeks.

"Rudy, you here? I wanna show you my dance for the compet…"

"Mary, shhhh. Papa isn't feeling well. I finally got him to lay down for a nap."

Frustration lined her face and tears welled up in her eyes.

"Is everything okay?" I asked scared by her solemn behavior.

"Of course, now what is it that you wanted to show me?" Rudy asked quickly trying to hide the truth about Papa's health. He had been diagnosed with dementia seven years ago. In denial about his illness, he refused any help that the family offered him. He was a strong man, and he refused to be seen as anything else. But when he couldn't remember the names of his beloved children, or where he had been only minutes before, Rudy lovingly stepped in to take care of her aging grandfather. She knew that he would have done it for her, so she and her husband Parker packed up their lives and moved into Papa's spacious two-story home. There was plenty of room in the old house, but Parker missed

The Icing On Top Ain't Always Sweet

having his own. Over the years, Papa's condition worsened no matter how hard Rudy prayed for some sort of relief. You could see the burden in her eyes, but she refused to acknowledge it. He was her grandfather, and that was that. Rudy tended to keep his condition to herself, as she didn't want to place that burden on anyone else.

"You're crying. Tell me. I can handle it. It's about Papa, huh?" I pressed.

"The doctor said that he's catching pneumonia. Fluid is filling his lungs faster than his body can respond. He was been getting sicker and sicker by the day it seems."

"Well, let's get him to the hospital. They gotta be able to give him something to stop it," I hurried to say.

"Mary, I wish..."

DING. DONG.

"Go get the door," Rudy said returning to Papa's room thankful for the needed distraction.

"But..."

"But nothing. We'll talk later, okay?"

"Okay," I said as I reluctantly walked down the stairs. I was irritated that Rudy continued to treat me as a child. I had done and seen a lot of things in my short 17 years of life, but she still tried to shelter me from the truth. But that was impossible because no matter what, life's coldhearted reality always seemed to find me.

"Who is it?" I asked opening the front door. When I looked up, it was the last person I expected to see. "Denise?"

"Hey, Mary, I was hoping that I would find you over here," my estranged older sister said beaming with excitement. It had been months since I had spoken to her. My father's oldest daughter, 18 years my senior, was constantly in-and-out of our lives. I always dreamt about us having a real sister-sister relationship, but every time I reached out to her, I was always disappointed. Denise's story was similar to my own. She didn't have a great relationship with our father, and her mother wasn't around either. Denise did what she could to survive. From selling drugs to taking off her clothes for money, Denise made it on her own. But many of her choices led her straight down the path to jail. Each time she would get out, she would tell our dad that she was finished living that type of lifestyle, and she was ready to clean her life up. I don't know if it was because he heard it so many times before, but he never had the faith that she would. And I couldn't blame him.

"Can I talk to you?"

I looked back up the stairs and heard nothing but silence. I knew that Rudy was probably reading Papa's favorite book to him again, so I had a few moments to spare.

"We can talk out here," I said pointing outside to the porch. Denise sat down on the steps, and I quickly followed behind her.

"What are you doing here?" I questioned.

"Hello to you too," she said sucking her teeth, "I came to see you and Dad."

"For?"

"Do I have to have a reason to see my family?"

"No, but when you get out of jail two months ago, I have to ask myself why you're here?"

"I know, and I'm sorry. I wanted to see you, but when I called Dad, I didn't think that he wanted to see me."

"You're his daughter. Of course he wants to see you."

"Well, he didn't seem that enthusiastic when I called."

I knew that in the past, Denise and our father had a rocky relationship, but if we were able to mend ours, I knew there was hope for them too. She just had to give our family a chance.

"Listen, I know that you and Dad haven't always seen eye-to-eye, but he's really not that bad. I mean look what he's done for me."

"You don't know him like I do, Mary. Do you think he was Mr. MLK when I was growing up? No. He was constantly chasing women and either leaving me at home alone to fend for myself or at a stranger's house without him."

"Why do you always do this?"

"Do what, Mary? I'm just trying to be honest."

"You're jealous, aren't you?"

"Jealous? Jealous of what?" Denise asked standing up. The sun was shining in her face, but I could still see the hurt in her eyes.

"Me and Dad are finally getting to a good place. I understand that he made some mistakes in the past, but that was the past. He is a different man now."

"Why do you always put him on a pedestal? He's going to let

you down exactly how he let me down. He doesn't know how to be anything other than a disappointment."

"Well, you would know," I said getting up, "Bye, Denise." As I walked back into the house, I kicked myself for even entertaining Denise. She only wanted people to feel sorry for her, but her tricks didn't work on me anymore. Art taught me how to deal with her from a distance. He would always say, "You can hang with her, just don't be anything like her."

***

Two weeks later, my family was gathered together around my grandfather's bed. Early the night before, he passed in his sleep. Rudy had an almost eerie sense of calmness of her face, but she knew that he was in a better place. He would always tell his children that a man without a mind of his own was no man at all, and we all knew that it pained him to have to deal with the dementia continuing to take over. He was losing control, and he knew that he would never get it back. While everyone said silent prayers for my Papa's safe journey home, I cried like a baby. My grandfather was just another person who I had to add to the list of people I'd lost. I thought that after George was murdered that I would become immune to the sting of death's touch around me, but each time hurt like the first. I missed him already.

"You hungry?" Rudy asked me hoping to do anything to make me feel better. I could barely stop crying; I didn't know how she expected me to eat.

"No—thank you," I stuttered.

The sight of my grandfather peacefully lying in bed looked like he was in a dream that he didn't want to be wakened from. Unfortunately, I didn't feel the same. I had to get out of there. As I got up to leave, my dad's girlfriend Vanessa rolled her eyes as I passed. I ignored the rude gesture and headed for the door. I refused to allow her to make my Papa's death about her. As word spread that my grandpa died, many members of the community came to pay their respects. Cards, food, and condolences were all given to my dad, Rudy and Parker whom accepted them graciously. Not many were allowed upstairs, but Rudy made exceptions for certain members of his esteemed church.

Mz. Skittlez

"Excuse me, Sister Brannon," I said rushing past one of the choir directors.

"Mary, you're just the person I'm looking for. Your sister asked me to come find you."

"Denise is here?" I asked rolling my red, puffy eyes.

"I was downstairs straightening up for Rudy when she came."

"Thank you, Sister Brannon." I was annoyed that Denise insisted on keeping drama in our family. Our grandfather just passed, and I did not want to upset the family any further.

"What is it now, Denise?" I asked while grabbing a tissue from the small box of Kleenex that sat on the table next to me.

"I'm so sorry," she said throwing her arms around me. This was the first time that she had ever hugged me that hard. I froze up from the unfamiliar feeling. "I never meant to hurt you guys. I am still dealing with hurts from my past, but that's no reason to take it out on you. I want to rebuild our relationship. You're my sister, and I love you. When I got the call about Papa, I fell to my knees. I never got to tell him how much he meant to me, and now it's too late. I don't want it to be too late for us."

As much as I wanted to send her back wherever it is she came from, she was my big sister, and of course, I loved her. I used to dream about what it would be like to be close, sharing secrets, talking about boys. Even though she was older than I was, she had been through a lot growing up, and I used to think that she would be able to help me make sense of it all, but I now I knew that she was just as lost as I was.

After everyone left, my grandpa's body was taken to the hospital. My dad, Vanessa, Rudy, Parker, Denise, and I stayed behind to discuss his last wishes.

"Two funerals?" my dad asked with confusion covering his face, "But he only has one body."

"That's what Papa always talked about. He wanted to have a simple service here in Cleveland, but he wanted to be buried in Garlin. That was his home."

My grandpa came from a small town in South Carolina, and that's where he planned to spend eternity right along with other members of the McKoy clan. My father couldn't argue with Rudy. He knew Papa's strong ties to his hometown, and he wanted nothing but the best for him.

"I'll make the call in the morning. It's been a long day, I'll see you all tomorrow," my father said grabbing Vanessa's hand who had hinted that she was ready to go, "Mary, you coming?"

"I think I'm gonna stay here," I said wanting to be around Rudy and Apples. I knew that my dad and Vanessa were just going to leave me alone anyway, but I needed to be around those who loved me. I wanted to be in my grandfather's house.

***

Three days later, I found myself in the back of a silver and black hearse. The sadness that filled the car could be felt for miles. I watched as Rudy poured her heart out into the tissue she held tightly in her hand. The reality of Papa truly being gone didn't hit her until she set foot into the car. After making sure that the casket was set for Garlin, and the flowers and food were perfect for the memorial, Rudy only hoped in her heart that Papa would be pleased with her efforts. She didn't want to say goodbye, but if she had to, she wanted to do it right. Denise had made it a point to stay by my side through it all. It was unlike her, but I appreciated that she was trying. She was a part of our family, so it was only right that she be there. Papa wouldn't have wanted it any other way.

As we arrived at the morgue for the memorial service, a few people gathered out in front. Many stopped my father and Rudy in their tracks to tell them how great my grandfather was, and how much he touched their lives. Rudy was pleased by the vast amount of love and admiration he received. She was honored. After the family spoke a few words, Rudy opened the floor to those in attendance. We spent hours telling our favorite stories of Papa. The building was filled with laughter, love, and lost moments. I was at peace as I felt my grandfather's presence in the room. He was another one of my guardian angels. Before the service was over, I walked to the front and, I grabbed a microphone from the stand and slowly approached the stage. I stared at my father and let the words flow from my mouth.

What do you do when you've done all you can, and it seems like it's never enough? And what do you do you say when your friends turn away, and you're all alone? Tell me, what do you do when you're giving your all, and it seems like you can't make it through? Well, you just stand when there's nothing left to do…

As I finished Donnie McClurklin's "Stand," I could tell that everyone was moved. When I returned to my seat, my dad kissed me on top of my head. No words were spoken, but that small gesture was good enough for me.

"Thank you for coming. The actual burial service will be down in Garlin, South Carolina. Papa wanted to be buried at home, so that's where he'll be," Rudy said informing the last guest to leave. Many were disappointed that they wouldn't be part of his final send off, but they understood and respected his wises.

"I can't go to that," Denise said standing in the middle of the foyer, "I thought that we were just having a viewing and a burial. I'm sorry. I didn't know that it was all the way in South Carolina. I can't afford to go."

"Girl, don't be silly. We're family. We got you," Rudy said wanting to reassure her.

"It's okay, Rudy, I was able to say my goodbyes today, so that's what was most important."

"I have an idea," Art said, "Why don't you cover me at the store while we're gone? I have some paperwork I need you to sign."

Not only was my father an active leader in the community, he was a proud business owner. With stores, barbershops, and a restaurant, he had his hands in a little bit of everything. Wanting to instill a little discipline and responsibility, Art made Denise a co-owner of his restaurant, but as she stayed in-and-out of trouble, he lost the faith that she could handle it. What should have been named *Denise's Kitchen* was soon named *Vanessa's Kitchen* in what Denise felt was out of spite. She was secretly proud of what our father was able to create and sustain all on his own, but she hated how Vanessa always seemed to take credit for his hard work.

"It'll be perfect," my dad began, "Denise, you manage everything and take care of the paperwork I need signed and Vanessa cooks. She's gonna stay back too."

"So no one cares that we are burying our grandfather?"

"Rudy, I need someone here to look after things. But two is even better," my father said patting Denise on the back. I was in awe of how genuine he seemed. I knew that he always took care of the logistics of his businesses. He was only giving Denise busywork in fear that she would cause a scene at the funeral and embarrass the family. She was being surprisingly cordial, but I knew that it would be only a matter of time before she was ready to rehash the past again. Or maybe I was wrong. Maybe I was wrong to assume the worst from her. Maybe this was her chance to prove us all wrong. I looked at the depression in her face, and I just wanted to see her smile. She had been through so much that I knew how she felt all too well. Once and for all, I wanted to see her finally win.

"We'll give your respects for you, Denise," I said smiling. I knew what it felt like to have no one believe in you. I didn't want to be that person to her.

"Well, it's set then. Well, be flying out in the morning. I expect you to be punctual tomorrow, Denise. I'll call you later and let you know what I need you to do."

"I got it, Dad," Denise said excited about the opportunity. Since she had been released from jail, she was on a mission to turn her life around. As easy as it was to go down the wrong path, and revert back to her old ways, she wanted something different. She needed something different. She wanted to prove to the world that she didn't have to be a screw-up for the rest of her life. There was still hope for her.

"Vanessa, if you need anything, call Denise," Art said before walking his beloved girlfriend outside of the mortuary.

***

The flight to South Carolina was long and draining. I had always dreamt of what it would be like when I took my first plane ride. I always thought that I would be on my way to a photo shoot or music video. Although I knew that my Papa's death was inevitable, it was never real to me. I had cried all my pain out for my grandfather, so I held Rudy as she had held me and let her tears paint my shirt with her grief. Even though she was happily married to Parker, she knew that she hadn't invested her all into their marriage. Many times, she neglected him to care for Papa, but it was a sacrifice that she was willing to make. But now with him gone, she didn't know where she fit in it all. She had spent years confiding in him, telling him her hopes, fears, and dreams without judgment. Who would she lean on now? When we arrived in Garlin, one of my father's many cousins picked us up from the airport. He drove down a long dirt road that was surrounded by nothing but trees. The mixture of fresh air and dirt filled my lungs. In Cleveland, there was no fresh air, so the change was needed.

"Dad, are we almost there yet," I asked uncomfortable in the old '67 Cadillac that looked like it was headed for nowhere. The ripped seats stabbed the back of my thighs causing red marks to form with each bump we hit in the road.

"Almost, Mary. Practice patience…"

Ring. Ring. Ring. Ring.

My dad's old-school ringtone echoed in the large metal car.

"Hello? Vanessa, slow down. I can't understand you—slow down. She what?"

I saw my father's face flush bright red as he continued his conversation with Vanessa.

"You stay away from Denise, and tell her that I said to stay away from you. I really can't deal with this right now, Vanessa. Can you promise not to kill each other before I get back? I'm just asking for a few days, okay? And when I get back, we'll figure this all out. I promise."

I nosily sat up trying to hear the other side of the conversation. All I could hear was Vanessa screaming in the background, but I couldn't make out her words.

"Dad, what happened?" I asked becoming uneasy by his silence.

"Your sister happened. That's what happened?" he said through his teeth.

"What…"

"We'll talk about it later," he said turning around in his seat. From the look on his face, I knew not to press the issue.

My father's mostly deaf, older cousin was oblivious to the tension in the car. He was just happy to be out and about. His simple, country life kept him contently isolated, but sometimes, it was nice seeing fresh faces.

"We're here," Cousin James said through his tinted false teeth.

It wasn't the glamorous place I imagined I would be flying to. The modest two-bedroom home fit James perfectly. It had been in their family for years. My grandfather grew up there as well, so it was nice to see where he came from. My father dragged our bags from the trunk as he woke up Rudy. She had cried so much that her body had no energy left to function. She passed out five minutes into the ride.

"What I miss?" she asked wiping the remaining sleep from her eyes.

"Denise attacked Vanessa," my father said furiously. I walked out of the house as the words left his mouth.

After Vanessa and Denise made it to the store to open for the day, their attitudes became apparent. Denise felt like the restaurant was her business. Her name was on the paperwork, so why wasn't it named after her. Once Denise saw how Vanessa operated, her patience grew thin. Dad put her in charge, and she planned to whip that place into shape. But Vanessa didn't take orders from anyone, not even my father. When Vanessa wouldn't comply with her way of doing things, Denise rushed into the kitchen where Vanessa continued to spew insults. She went into Art's office and grabbed the small lox-box that he kept his earnings from the night before. She filled a large box with things from around the restaurant. Some were seemingly insignificant, but Denise felt like they were of utmost importance to get her point across.

"Where do you think you're going? I'm calling Art right now," Vanessa said pulling her cell phone out of her white apron.

Denise didn't say a word as she ran past Vanessa with the box spilling over. Instead of calling my father, Vanessa decided to call the authorities. She was tired of people walking all over her. If neither she nor Art could control Denise then she would allow the only people who could.

"Hello? I would like to report a robbery."

***

It had almost been a week since Denise and Vanessa got into it. My father was furious when he got home. Vanessa did her best to straighten up the restaurant, but when he got there, he could tell what was missing. Denise has taken mostly his stuff after all.

"Has she called yet?" I pressed my dad. I knew that she was probably embarrassed, but she had to show up sooner or later.

"No, but you know how your sister is." I knew that deep down he was hurt even though he would never show it. My father regretted not being the best to neither Denise, nor me but he didn't know how to be any other way. Art was a valued member of our community, and he was held to a higher standard, so he held that same standard to us.

"I think she would have shown up by now, Dad. I mean it's been over a week," I pleaded. Something wasn't right, and I was determined to get to the bottom of things. While my dad walked around the restaurant doing an inventory of what was missing, I continued to call Denise's phone, but each time, I was sent to voicemail.

"Okay, Denise, this isn't funny anymore. Please just call us back and let us know you are okay at least. It was just a misunderstanding," I said wanting to reassure her. Just as the last words left my lips, my phone rang. When Denise's phone number popped up on the screen, I breathed out a sigh of relief.

"Denise, where have you…"

"Hi, Mary, this Joe," Denise's roommate slowly said into the phone.

"Where is Denise?"

Joe agreed to let Denise stay with him while she was getting on her feet. He worked nights, so he and Denise constantly missed each other. When she was there, he was asleep and vice versa, but Denise was thankful for his help nonetheless.

"I was hoping to ask you the same thing. I was at work, and she called and said that her car was stolen. She was really upset about it. She kept talking about some box."

I knew that she was probably talking about the stuff she had stolen form the restaurant. Her disappearance was only to cover up her embarrassment of stealing from our dad.

"Did she say anything else?" I questioned.

"I told her to call the police and file a police report and that I would be home from work in the morning. She sounded pretty shook up, so I offered to leave work early, but she told me not to. She said that she was the one responsible, so she had to deal with it. When I came home, her clothes were laid out on the bed, her phone was on the nightstand, the TV was still on, so I knew that she had been home. It was like she just vanished. I've been here all day, but she hasn't been back yet. I think you all should call the police."

I could hear the concern in Joe's voice, and it only added to my own anxiety. I knew that something was just not right.

"Thanks, Joe, call me if you hear anything," I said rushing to find my dad.

"My gun is gone. My gun is gone," I heard him continue to say.

"Dad..."

"What does she need with a gun?" my father questioned.

"Dad," I yelled snapping him back from his thoughts, "Denise is missing."

"Missing?"

"Joe called and said that Denise called him and said that her car was stolen. There was a box in it," I said waiting for a reaction. My father was smart, so he knew that all of his possessions were long gone.

"Just give it a few more days, Mary. She'll turn up. I know it," he said clearing off his desk.

***

And wait a few days we did. By this time, it had been two weeks since Vanessa and Denise had their altercation. After Vanessa called the police, she embellished the story in her favor. She cried to the police officer who was taking down the report and said that Denise attacked her in a jealous rage.

"This is her father's establishment. I can't help what he wants to name it," she said for the record.

After I spoke with Joe, my dad began to worry.

"Dad, it's been two weeks. We have to do something," I snapped. I hadn't slept in days. My conscience wouldn't let me forget about my sister.

"Dad!"

"If it'll make you feel better, we can go by her place, okay?"

If she wasn't there, I didn't see how that would make me feel better, but it was better than nothing was, I guessed. Thirty minutes later, I found myself parked right in front of Denise's apartment. The shaded street was almost hidden at the end of the empty block. I quickly walked up to the front door that led to Denise's apartment and rang the buzzer to her unit, but there was no answer.

"Denise," I yelled up to the third floor. Her window appeared cracked, but my voice went unheard. I buzzed the door again. Still nothing.

My dad pulled a spare key out from his pants' pocket and opened the door. I impatiently followed behind him as we ascended the stairs. A few flights later, we finally found her apartment. As my dad was opening the door, I stared down the hall at a large stained-glass window. The shaded trees outside constantly surrounded the apartment, so no light was ever allowed to illuminate the beautiful colored panels, which sat at the end of the hall. It was still pretty to look at.

"It looks like no one has been here in days," I heard my father say.

Denise's belongings were exactly where Joe said they were. He had been arrested a few days before. When Vanessa made the police report, my father followed through with it in hopes that he would be able to obtain some of his missing property. The police did a full investigation, and Joe was arrested as an accomplice. The police figured that since they lived together that Joe had to be in on it as well. I felt bad that Joe was a victim of circumstances, but finding Denise was still my number one priority.

"Something is wrong, Dad. I can feel it."

Frustrated, I walked back out into the hall toward the same stained glass window I had been admiring earlier. I looked at all of the various colors as I began to pray to the only one whom could guide me. I leaned on the back of a high-backed chair as my plea began.

"God, I know that Denise has made some mistakes, but please let her be okay. I want to be a sister to her. I just don't know how. So many things have distanced us in the past, but I'm begging for another chance to get it right this time. I don't want to give up on her like everyone else had in the past. I believe that people can do amazing things. You're still working on me, God, so I know that someone can change for the better. Please just let me find my sister." My heart was heavy, and I felt my chest getting tighter. My asthma was acting up again. Just as I was about to sit down in the big, comfy chair that sat next to the window, I heard, "Mary, let's go."

I got up and took one last look at the window.

"Let's go down to the station," my dad said holding Denise's cell phone in his hand. With every day that passed, he began to worry more and more. Hoping that God had time to answer one last prayer, I followed behind my dad.

8

"When someone you love becomes a memory...the memory becomes a treasure."

After going downtown to file a missing person's report, word got out that Art McKoy's daughter was missing. New crews surrounded the station even before the ink even had a chance to dry on the page. I was used to being in the spotlight competing in different pageants and talent shows, but this was a whole new form of attention. The flashing lights blinded me as we walked out. Loud continuous clicks were all that could be heard on top of, "Mr. McKoy, do you have any idea where your daughter is?"

"She's been gone for two weeks. Why are you just now reporting her missing?" another reporter rudely asked.

"A press conference will be held later today. All questions will be addressed at that time," my father said bypassing the crowd with me in hand. He became a pro at the media game. As many people who loved and adored him, there were just as many who hated him. Reporters would constantly hound him in regards to his political agenda, but my father stood strong in his convictions, so he learned how to keep the vultures at bay. But the sight of the huge crowd sent chills down my spine. This was no longer a game. Denise was in trouble, and we had to help her.

Later that day, my father held a small press conference back at Denise's apartment. Before I watched my father send his plea out into the world, the Police Chief spoke.

"Good evening, today the Cleveland Police Department will do its best to provide the public with the information on a missing woman from our community, Denise McKoy. This investigation will remain a very serious concern and a huge priority for our department. I would like to thank the volunteers of the Black Crime Organization for assisting law enforcement and the McKoy family at this time. I will now turn over the mic to the victim's father, Mr. Arthur McKoy."

"Two weeks ago, my eldest daughter Denise McKoy disappeared. Her 2002 Honda Civic car was stolen from right in front

The Icing On Top Ain't Always Sweet

of her house, and she has not been seen since. She's 5'5", brown skin, dark hair," my father said holding up a picture of Denise to the camera, which sat, right in front of him, "If anyone has seen my daughter, please contact the Cleveland Police Department. Denise, if you're out there and see this, please just know that we love you, and you want to see you home." I stood behind my dad in solidarity. We were going to find Denise, no matter how long it took. Once my father finished, it was my turn to plead to the camera. I asked the community to assist in any way they could. I prayed that someone anyone had seen Denise. It was our only chance.

  After the press conference was over, I was mentally exhausted to say the least. I just wanted to sleep. I went home with Rudy needing to be home with Apples. Her small, innocent nature soothed me. I had to turn my mind off. I was going crazy. My father had police escorts follow us home and they let us know that they would be there, as long they needed to be. I hated feeling as if I had no privacy, but the way things were going, I couldn't be too careful.

  The next morning, I woke up exceptionally early. I heard several people talking downstairs, so I threw on my robe, and headed to see what the commotion was about.

  "Art, my guys are doing everything they can to find your daughter. You have to trust me. There was something weird back at the apartment. There's no forced entry. Nothing was taken, but somehow Denise just disappears. There has to be something we're missing. The roommate's story checks out, but if Denise called him the night before she disappeared then there has to be a reason why she would have left so suddenly like that."

  "Well, if you think it will help to go back, let's go," my father said, "Let me just grab my coat."

  "I'm coming too," I interrupted. There was no way he was going to leave me behind. If the police thought we should go back to Denise's then I wanted to be there looking for her right along with them.

  Less than an hour later, we arrived in front of Denise's. I had been there more times in the last week then I had ever been in my life. The sun light couldn't permeate the thick shade that surrounded the complex, so we just sat in darkness.

"You wait out here. I'll be right back," my father instructed as he got out of the car. I watched as he unlocked the door that led inside while the police chief walked alongside him.

I quietly prayed that they found something anything, and at that moment, unknowingly, my wish came true. Suddenly, six other police officers rushed inside the apartment building. You would have thought that the building was on fire, the way they ran in. I jumped out of the car eager to see anything they found that would bring us one step closer to finding Denise.

Before I could get inside the door, a burly, young officer came down the stairs pushing me back outside. "You can't go in there, Mary."

"Why not?" I barked, "My dad is in there. Now move."

The officer didn't budge as I did my best to get inside. I had to know what was going on, but he closed the door behind him locking me out.

"Where's my dad?" I banged and screamed until my dad came downstairs.

Art came walking out of the house with his eyes staring down at the floor. "We found her."

"Where is she?" I asked, but he didn't answer.

The words didn't register. How did Denise have the gun? They must've found her. Not receiving the answers I needed from my dad, I rushed past him and the other officer and ran up the stairs like my life depended on it. When I got to Denise's floor, I saw the other cops standing by the same stained-glass window I had been just the day before. As I got closer, the smell in the air was unbearable. I saw what appeared to be a light gray blanket peeking out, and my steps quickened as hair and then a head revealed itself. It was Denise. Blood painted the side of her face, but her neat micro braids did their best to cover up the small hole in her head.

"No, no, no," I repeated. I fell to my knees at the sight of Denise's lifeless face. I had lost another person.

After Denise got home, she was furious at Vanessa. She hadn't liked her since day one, but she hated that she allowed Vanessa to send her over the edge. This was her one chance to prove to our father that she wasn't the same person anymore. She wanted to be better, but she failed again. After taking a shower, Denise grabbed the gun she had taken from the restaurant, her blanket, came out into the hallway, and thought about all the wrongs she couldn't make right. Growing up, Denise had been suicidal, but no one ever took her seriously. Unable to cope with the looming disappointment from our father, Denise decided that night that enough was enough. Grief stricken, she consumed countless drugs and a bottle of alcohol. It seemed like she couldn't get her life together even though she was trying. Once the effect of the drugs kicked in, she took the gun and placed it close to her temple. The cold sensation of the gun made her hesitate, but she didn't have any other choice. She was tired of the pain. She just wanted to rest. As she closed her eyes, she pulled the trigger and escaped from everything that held her to this world.

    The forensic autopsy report concluded that Denise had indeed committed suicide. After she shot herself, her body slumped down, and the gun fell between her legs. The cover she adorned draped over her decomposing body, and her braids covered the wound she so selfishly created. The police were in awe that no one in the building heard or reported the gun shot that was fired so close to their own doors.

    Denise's homecoming service was beautiful. Rudy made sure that her dress was nice and pressed, and that the flowers were positioned just right. While the service continued, and the choir sang, my father couldn't help but to blame himself. The fight between Vanessa and Denise was so menial. He just wished that he had the chance to talk to her before she made such a final decision. He regretted not reaching out to her and letting her know how much he loved her. It was a regret that he would carry with him for the rest of his life. I didn't know if it would do much, but when the choir finished, I crept up to the front and spoke with the funeral director. I had to give it a try. I performed a ballet number in my sister's honor. Dance was one of my many gifts, and I wanted to share that with her. I let her memory flow through me as I moved. I knew that she was looking down on me, and I just wanted her to know that she was loved.

***

    After Denise's death, I felt myself going down the same dark path I had seen so many times before, but I didn't want to fall. I had to pick myself up.

"I want to do Miss Black USA," I said showing Rudy an invite I had received for the competition.

"Really? I thought that you were done with pageants?" she asked as she continued to fold the basket of clothes that sat on the couch next to her.

"I was never done. I just got bored, I guess. I mean I've already won the city, county, and state title here, the next step would have to be Miss Black USA."

After everything that had happened with my sister and Papa, I needed something to pick my spirits back up, and I knew that putting my all back into the pageant world would do the trick. I would be able to be back out in front of a crowd again, and that's where I wanted to be.

"I say go for it, Mary. You've won first place and *Miss Congeniality* in all of the pageants so far. You got this one."

Cousin Rudy always encouraged me to follow my dreams. With her confidence in me mixed with my desire to be in the spotlight again, I enrolled in the Miss Black USA pageant in Jacksonville, Florida. The competition was only a week away, but I knew I didn't need that much time to get ready. Competing was in my blood, so my performance had always been on point. After a few rehearsals, I would be good to go. I decided to dance for the talent portion. The piece I had been working on for weeks prior to Denise's suicide burned in my soul. It was perfect.

The day before the competition, a luncheon was held for all of the contestants. The winner from the year before spoke to us about her experience. During her reign, she had taken the opportunity to volunteer to help showcase the great work that the Miss Black USA organization did for the black community. The idea of instilling positive self-esteem in young girls was a mission for them all, and she was just as proud to spread that message. I looked up at her as she stood at the podium with her crystal blue gown, long, natural black hair, and her flawless milk-chocolate skin and saw myself. Not because we looked similar, but because I knew that, I could be an example to so many young girls as well. After the luncheon, there was a small meet and greet. The flood of bedazzled, pink shirts filled the room. Quickly I walked around and introduced myself to my fellow competition. The girls ranged from the lightest of lights to the darkest of darks, and I loved to see the rainbow of black women who were representing their states. But I was there to win. As I continued to work the room, I met a girl named Jessica. She was from New York, and her talent was singing. I clicked with her instantly.

"So what song are you singing?" I asked.

"'Amazing Grace,'" Jessica said proudly.

"Oh, that's nice." It was nice song, but it was typical. I knew that my dance had to win the judges over. It was an original contemporary piece, so I knew it would set me a part.

The next day, I arrived to the competition a little early. Rudy and Apples stayed back at the hotel getting ready. I was too anxious to wait. I was ready for my crown. When I walked inside, I was amazed by how big the stage area was. I looked out into the audience, and there had be at least three times more seats than any of my previous pageants. I felt little butterflies suddenly float around in my stomach. "I got this," I assured myself over and over again. I was used to being on stage. This was my time to shine.

I went backstage to get dressed for our opening number. We had been practicing a routine to Beyoncé's "Déjà Vu." I was excited because it was just another way for me to show the judges one of the many things I did best. Even though the routine had us dancing in unison, I was determined to hit the moves just a little harder than the girls beside me. I had to stand out. Winning Miss Black USA 2006 would be the ending I needed before college. The spotlight quickly danced across the stage; the show was about to begin. As all forty of us walked out in bright matching red, mini princess dresses with Swarovski crystals illuminating the front, the music began to play, and I was in my zone. With every note that played, I smiled as if my life depended on it, and every move we made, we made together. I looked out into the crowd and saw Rudy and Apples. Rudy was holding her, and I could see the excitement in her eyes. I wanted to be an example for her. Despite what Cash went through, I wanted to teach Apples that there was so much more to life, and that she could pursue her dreams no matter what they were. At that moment, I realized how strong I was and had always been. From the verbal and mental abuse from my mother, to losing all those I held close to me, I had persevered. I could have let those situations to break me down, but God allowed me to use them to build me back up. I was destined for greatness, and at that moment, I finally felt it.

    After the dance routine ended, we all ran back stage to change. After the interview portion would be Talent, and that's what I was waiting for. Once I began to pursue my creative path again and embrace who I really was, I became comfortable talking in front of others. In a wind of red, sparkly dresses being thrown around the room, I hurried to change looks. I threw on my Chanel inspired button down blazer and my mid-length skirt and prepared my answers. I looked at myself in the mirror and admired my handy work. I was sure no one would know the difference. I had to compete with these girls, so I wanted to look expensive. As I draped a diamond necklace that Rudy insisted, I use for the competition around my neck; I saw a glimpse of blue in my hair. In dim lighting, it appeared black. I wanted to be conservative in front of the judges while leaving a hint of blue to showcase my personality. When my turn came, I walked out on stage with an air of confidence that I had never seen in myself before. My gut was telling me that I had already won. I had never lost before, so there was no reason not to trust my instinct. Everything was perfect, and suddenly my nerves went away. After each girl was asked such questions as, "What does success mean to you?" or "If you could change one thing in the world, what would it be and why?" the judges quickly began to take note. Some girls let their nerves get the best of them as the stumbled through each question, but I held my head up high. I answered every question with a big smile and great posture while keeping my eyes on the judges. I felt strong in my performance. When I walked off stage, Jessica whispered, "Wish me luck," as she approached the crowd. She would need it.

    After the interviews came the talent portion of the show. I saw the pride in Rudy and Apples' faces as I peered from behind the curtain, which hid the last minute rehearsals. I put my headphones on and let the music take me away. At that moment, no one or nothing mattered. After I practiced for a few minutes, I began to hear the other girls as they each performed their title winning talent. One girl played the piano while another performed an amazing baton routine. I watched more and more as my turn quickly approached. I was mesmerized. The

The Icing On Top Ain't Always Sweet

talent definitely outshined what I had seen at the city or county level, but I knew that state prepared me. Here I was at the Miss Black USA pageant representing my home state of Ohio. I had to do my family proud. The girl who performed before me opted to do a rendition of "The Swan." With her tutu and all, I knew that my contemporary piece was going to kill it.

"Next we have Miss Ohio, Miss Mary McKoy dancing a contemporary number she choreographed herself," the pageant announcer said.

Applause quickly filled the room as I took my spot center stage. Musiq Soulchild's "Love" echoed throughout the room, and I let my body speak the words. I flowed through every move capturing the audience with every turn. My heart sang along with the song. I let all of my pain out on that stage as I arabesqued underneath the spotlight. All the loss and hurt I had ever felt poured onto the stage. Tears filled my eyes because I knew that so many angels were looking down upon me. When the music ended, I felt my light return. I was exactly where I needed to be. Entertaining a crowd was where my heart belonged, but winning Miss Black USA would be the icing on top.

By the end of my performance, I received a standing ovation. I knew that there were a couple of performances left, but I was ready for the crown. As I walked backstage, I passed by Jessica once again.

"Good luck," I said to her this time. I assumed she thought that she would seal the deal by performing a classic, but to me, it was a little boring. I had seen the faces of the judges when I performed, and I just didn't think that "Amazing Grace" would be able to compete with that.

"Please welcome Miss New York to the stage. She has a real treat for you all. Tell the people what you'll be performing tonight."

"Hello, my name is Jessica Harris. I am 17-years old, and I will be performing 'Amazing Grace.' This song is a song that I grew up listening to. My grandmother would sing it to me almost every night, but she would sing it to me in Spanish because she is of Panamanian decent. This exposure to Spanish at such an early age created my passion for learning. So over the years, I have become fluent in five other languages—French, Spanish, Italian, Cantonese, and Japanese. So in honor of my grandmother and also to highlight my personality tonight, I will be performing the song in all five languages."

"That is truly amazing, Jessica."
As Jessica walked up to the mic, my mouth dropped open.

Amazing Grace, dont le son doux. Cela a sauvé un misérable comme moi. J'étais perdu, mais maintenant je suis trouvé. J'étais aveugle, mais maintenant je vois. T'was grâce qui a enseigné mon coeur à la crainte. Et Grace, mes craintes soulagés. Comment précieux n'a que Grace semble/L'heure j'ai cru d'abord...

She looked beautiful. At that moment, I knew that the competition was now between Jessica and me. We both had the best performances of the night by far. There were a lot of good contestants, but the only thing that stood in my way of winning the title was the swimsuit competition. It took me a little while to get comfortable with my body, and strangely enough, Swimsuit always helped me do that. Rudy would say that I was advertising the bathing suit and not my body, so that's what I did. After dazzling the crowd and the judges in a bright purple, sequin two-piece, it was then time for the crowning ceremony. Each girl hurried to change into her final outfit of the night. My long white, ball gown glittered under the lighting. I had spent days getting it just right.

As we all walked out in unison and took our places on the stage, I looked down at my 'Miss Ohio' sash I wore. I was ready to be crowned Miss Black USA 2006. It was only fitting.

"And *Miss Congeniality* goes to Miss Texas."

I was surprised that my name wasn't called. In all my other pageants, I had won *Miss Congeniality* along with the title every time, but I told myself that it was a small sacrifice for the crown.

"*Prettiest Smile* goes to Miss Colorado."

One by one, the awards were being giving out, and I hadn't placed yet. But the crown was still on the line, so I was convinced that it had my name written all over it. As the final award was given out, the announcer prepared to crown the winner as he held the 'Miss Black USA' sash in hand.

"Congratulations to the 2006 Miss Black USA winner…"

Before the name even left his mouth, I began to walk forward. I mean why delay the inevitable?

The Icing On Top Ain't Always Sweet

"...Jessica Harris!" the announcer continued.

The words didn't register as I walked to the front of the stage. A smile spread across my face. I had assumed he said, "Mary" until the stage director quickly pulled me to the side. I watched as Jessica graciously accepted her crown oblivious to my blatant assumption of winning. While the announcer placed the crown on her head, I felt the room spin, and then suddenly everything went black.

***

As Rudy lightly splashed water across my face, I realized I was lying on the floor. The beautiful gown I had spent hours on was ruined. Small speckles of dirt stuck to it as I hurried to brush them off. In the mist of Jessica becoming the Miss Black USA, I fainted. Luckily, the stage director caught me before I fell off the stage, but I was still embarrassed. As the show's EMT did a quick examination, I could not believe that I had lost. I was just as talented as Jessica was if not more. The show had to be rigged. All of the hard work that I had put in meant nothing anymore. I was done. At that moment, I didn't care if I competed in another one ever again. I just wanted to go home, and get out of that stupid dress.

Rudy and Apples hurried back stage to make sure that I was okay.

"Are you hurt?" she asked wiping my face with a tissue.

"No, I'm fine. Just drop it okay." I was too embarrassed to talk about it.

"No, not okay, Mary. You fainted," Rudy said. I could see the concern on her face.

"I'm ready to go," I said leaving the stage. I brushed past the other girls and headed for the exit. Before I got to the back door, I had to squeeze past Jessica as she answered questions in a sea of cameras. Lights continued to flash as they captured her moment. I looked at her crown and hated every crystal that glittered. I had more important things to tend to than some simple competition, so I took one last glance, and I never looked back.

***

After losing Miss Black USA, I began to focus more on college. Being in the last semester of my senior year, I had prom and graduation coming up. Rudy was constantly reminding me. I think that she was more excited than I was. After getting all glitzed and glammed up for the pageant, I had no energy to get ready for prom, so I began to stay at my dad's house a little more. I just needed a time out, and that's what I got there unless Vanessa was home. We had never seen eye-to-eye. I don't think she got along with anyone in our family, but she seemed to pick on me the most. One day after school, I went home and went downstairs to the basement. I tried to stay out of Vanessa's way for my own sake, and she barely went down there, so it was perfect. After watching TV for a while, I drifted off to sleep. It was hot outside, so the heat had me knocked out. Suddenly, I heard Vanessa yelling like something was on fire.

"Mary…Mary!" she continued to yell.

Before I could open my eyes all the way, she flew down the stairs. "Didn't I ask you to do those dishes?"

"What dishes?" I asked wiping my face.

"I swear, you and your father are just alike. It's not my job to clean up after you. You are not my child, and you are almost 18-years old at that."

"You never asked me to do any dishes, Vanessa." I didn't want to fight, but I was tired of her blaming everything on. It was like nothing was ever good enough for her. If she wasn't yelling at my father, she was yelling at me,

"I shouldn't have to ask you, Mary. That's the problem now. You don't contribute. Your father doesn't make you lift a finger, and then I become the bad guy when I ask you to do anything. I run my house a certain way, Mary, and if you can't…"

"Fine, I'll wash the dishes," I said getting up. I knew she just wanted to argue, and I didn't want to be a part of it. I had enough on my mind as it was.

"No, I'm tired of having this conversation with you. You're just like your father. You're never gonna change."

"What are you saying?"

"I'm saying you have to find another place to live. I am done. I've already talked to Art."

I was speechless. Here I was a senior in high school, and I was being kicked out of my father's house. I wondered why he didn't stand up for me. Where was I supposed to go? I knew that I could always go back with Rudy, Parker, and Apples, but I was tired of depending on them for everything. Apples would be good until I was able to get on my own two feet. They treated her like their own, so I knew I did not have to worry. I owed a lot to them, and I wanted to show them that they taught me how to be independent and get it on my own, and that's what I set out to do. Without saying another word, I went upstairs to pack up my clothes and called the only person I could think of—William. He had always been there for me when I needed him. And although he treated me like a sister, I knew it would be a lot to ask of him.

"What's up, Skittlez?" he asked answering on the first ring.
"My dad's girlfriend just kicked me out. I have nowhere to go."
"You need me to come get you?"
"Can you?"
"Yeah, I'm on my way right now."

9

"If it's important to you, you will find a way. If not, you will find an excuse."

After graduation, I moved in with my other friend A-Rod. William had been living with his mother, so I only stayed there for a few days. A-Rod knew someone who had an extra bedroom and who was willing to let me stay. Fresh out of high school with no money to my name, anywhere was better than nowhere. I started getting back into my music again, which helped a lot with the transition. I had only been gone a few weeks, and Art hadn't called to check on me once. I knew that whatever Vanessa said went, but he was still my father. He left me out in the cold, but I was determined to get back on my feet by myself. As I continued to do music, I found my purpose again. While I was still salty about losing the Miss Black USA competition, I then realized that all of the pageants I had been in were only preparing me for my first true love—music. I loved performing. I loved creating, and music allowed me to do both.

The summer before my freshmen year at Kent State University, I got a call from Art.

"I need you to do me a favor."

"Hello to you too Dad."

"Don't be like that, Mary," Art said hearing the frustration in my voice. It had been weeks since I had last spoken to him, and now out of the blue, he was calling to ask me for a 'favor.'

"Oh, I'm fine. Thanks for asking."

"Listen, I know that you're mad, but you're 18 now. You should be out on your own."

Not wanting to argue, I changed the subject. I knew that my father would never understand, and I didn't have the time to try to explain it to him.

"*The East Cleveland Love Fest* is coming up."

"Okay?"

"I need you to run it for me."

The Icing On Top Ain't Always Sweet

"I don't know anything about running a festival," I said panicking, "Why can't you do it?"

"Honestly, I've outgrown it, and plus, I want to pass it down to you, Mary. I need you."

One part of me wanted to leave my dad high and dry like he had left me, but I couldn't. That's what Vanessa probably expected too, and I wanted to prove them both wrong.

"When is it?" I asked reluctantly.

"Next week."

"Dad, that doesn't give me a lot of time."

"I basically got everything off the ground. I just need you to sign a couple contracts for me, secure a few of the vendors, and manage the booths and the talent."

"Is that all?" I asked sarcastically.

"Yep, you'll be fine." I knew that by doing this, I was helping Art out, but I intended to help myself in the process. He always put together a fun and successful festival, and money flooded the area as families of Cleveland enjoyed great fun, food, and entertainment.

A week later, I found myself running around like a chicken with its head cut off. I was able to manage the entire festival on my own. I don't know if it was from watching my father years before or just my natural instinct, but I thrived under the pressure. I even included a spot on stage to perform my music. The crowd was massive that day, so I knew that would be a great opportunity to showcase my skills and further get my name out there. I would be starting college soon, so I didn't know how much time I would have to perform.

***

A few days later, I met up with my father to give him the earnings from the festival, $20,000 cash. I had never seen so much money before in my life. By this time, I had been living with A-Rod and the owner of the house Chris for maybe a month. Rent was never an issue because Chris and A-Rod split it fifty-fifty anyway, and they knew that I was trying to get ready to start college in the fall, so whatever money I was able to save would be for school.

When I arrived at my dad's, I called his cell phone.

"Where you at?" he questioned.

"I'm outside."

"What you doing out there?" His confusion baffled me.

"Can we just talk out here please? I would just feel more comfortable." Not having to see Vanessa was my only goal.

"Here I come."

I waited on my father's porch as if I were a stranger. Minutes later, he opened the door eager to see how the festival went.

"So how'd you do?" he asked sitting on the swing that sat next to the front door.

"Huh," I said passing him a filled manila envelope which held crisp $100 bills.

Art looked inside as if expecting to see the amount. "Good job, Mary. I see things went well."

"They actually did. The food, activities, rides, and games all came together nicely. The lineup for the performances was packed."

"I heard you went on stage," Art said smiling slightly. As much as we didn't have the ideal father-daughter relationship, he was proud of me in his own way. He knew that if he gave me a task, I would follow through with it, and follow through I did.

"Well, here," he said handing me back $15,000.

"What's this for?" my eyes lit up like Christmas lights.

"It's your portion of the deal. You earned it, Mary. I know that you'll be starting Kent State in a few months, and I want you to have what you need while you're out there. You earned it."

I was shocked to say the least as I held the banded money together. Being that I was homeless, the money would help. Maybe the summer wouldn't be that bad after all.

***

After the festival, Chris started to notice my frequent purchases. I knew that Rudy and Parker were going to be helping me with school, but I wanted to lighten the burden as much as possible. As I walked into my room with a bag from Target filled with different items for my dorm room. I was happy that everything was coming together.

"Went shopping again, huh?" Chris asked peering into my room.

"Just got a few things for school," I said trying to ignore his intrusiveness.

"It seems like you been popping tags for weeks now."

"Uhn huhn," I said continuing to place the items in a large box I had in the closet.

"Listen, you gon have to start dropping on these bills. These lights aren't free," Chris said becoming annoyed. Over the summer, we hung out a few times, but I honestly felt obligated. Here I was living in his house rent free; it was the least I could do. With me doing my music and getting ready for Kent State, living with Chris and A-Rod was the only choice I had, but as much as I loved doing my music, I couldn't see myself paying rent for a place that was never mine. I had bigger plans.

"All of a sudden you want me to pay rent? Chris, you knew what my situation was when I first moved in…"

"Your situation looks a little different from this side," he said with skepticism dripping from his voice.

"Well, it's not. I'm not working right now, so the money I have is the only money I have to my name."

"If you're gonna be living here then you need to pull your own weight. I'm not in this relationship to have to take care of you," Chris snapped.

"Relationship? When was this ever a relationship? I thought we had been hanging out for the past few months, but not once did I feel like we were in a relationship. I see that I have been giving out the wrong signals, so maybe it's best for me to leave."

"Yeah, maybe," he said turning to leave. I knew his feelings were hurt, but the words needed to be said. I was only 18. I thought I had been in love before, but each time I realized that I wasted my love on the wrong people. Chris was a summer fling. I never wanted to take it any further than that. With me attending school in the fall, I was ready to meet new people and to experience new things, and being with Chris was never on the list.

After leaving Chris and A-Rod's house, I moved back in with Rudy and Parker. I had been coming to see Apples every day anyway, so it felt good to be back home. A few weeks before school started, I made sure that Apples had everything she needed as well. Rudy and Parker took great care of her, but she was my responsibility. We went shopping and had ice cream, and I spent my last days of summer drama free. It felt good for once.

"Are you sure you have everything?" Rudy asked nervous about the big change. I never told her about my summer at Chris'. She would have freaked. I knew that she would have accepted me back with open arms, but I wanted to do something for myself, and I was willing to sacrifice during the process.

When we walked into the dorm room, it was empty. My roommate hadn't arrived yet, so I was able to pick my side first. Of course, the place had no life about it, but that would change quickly. I would whip that place into shape in no time. Majoring in Fashion Merchandising with a double minor in Business Management and Marketing, I was ready to take my designs to the next level. What I had been teased about as a child was going to be the something that set me apart from the rest of my classmates. My eccentricness would be celebrated. While I was sad to see Rudy, Parker, and Apples leave, I was ready to open up the new chapter in my life. With all of my stuff moved in, I sat back and admired how far I had come. I worked to pull myself up from the bottom, but I knew that I was destined for so much more. With my first semester of classes looming ahead, I promised myself that this would be the best year yet, and boy was I right.

***

Two months into the semester, I had gotten used to being on my own. Living with Chris and A-Rod prepared me more than I knew at the time. I was so busy with schoolwork and pursuing my music, I had no time for anything else really, but I was fine with that. Anytime an opportunity presented itself for me to perform, I took it, no matter how hard it was.

One day while attending a campus event, I watched as several rappers and singers hit the stage. They were average at best, but the crowd loved them. Latif, a local event promoter, put out the hottest artists in the area. If his name was on the party then it was bound to sell out. Latif failed to disappoint because he loved what he did. He had an eye for talent, but for some reason, he didn't have his eye on me, but I was determined to change that.

"You should let me hit the stage," I said boldly.

"What?" Latif asked as he looked up from the seat he was sitting in.

"I'm an artist too. Mz. Skittlez."

The Icing On Top Ain't Always Sweet

"Yeah, I've heard of you," Latif said disinterested.

"Well, if you've heard of me then you know my performances never disappoint. Just check my track record," I said confidently, "If I don't rock the stage, I'll owe you. I'll promote for you for free if I have to."

I knew that Latif was the biggest promoter in the area, and if I wanted my music to be heard, he was the man to go to. Reluctantly, Latif allowed me to close the show. In my colorful fashion, I went on stage and let the music flow from my soul. Even though, I loved what I was learning in class, music would always be on my mind. I had a voice, and I was determined to let the world hear it. During my performance, I could see the amazement in Latif's eyes. He may have heard my name before, but during that moment, I showed him exactly who I was. After that day, Latif and I were inseparable business-wise. While he helped me to book different gigs to promote my music, I did club promoting for him on the side. It was a small price to pay for the amount of exposure I was able to get on a nightly basis. I had a pretty good following to start out with, but with Latif's connects, I was able to reach so many more people. Whenever I performed, the club would always sell out. It was hard to not see my name around town. My face was on every flyer for the hottest clubs in town, and once Latif saw how big my fan base had become, he was interested in investing into my music.

With his help, I opened up for Nicki Minaj, Wyclef, and Lil Scrappy just to name a few. Soon I found myself on tour, and school had taken a back seat. Luckily, my professors were able to see my ambition, and they encouraged it. I made sure to stay current on my assignments, but my attendance suffered because I was on the road a lot. In 2008, I was asked to be the opening act on BET's *Spring Bling*. During this time, music was the only thing on my mind. Maybe it was the loss I took at the Miss Black USA pageant, but I was determined to win. With a lot of late nights and early mornings, Latif helped me transition from college into the industry. At the young age of 19, I released my debut album *Sweet Tooth* and sold out shows all across the country. I had reached such a high level of success so fast that the rumors came faster. Many people began to think that Latif and I were dating. Like I said from the moment that he had heard me perform, we were inseparable, but it was strictly business. I looked at Latif as an older brother and a mentor, and I loved his wife and kids. Nothing romantic ever transpired between us. Truth be told, Latif looked at me like a little sister as well, so he used me to get close to all the other young girls around me. He was grown, so I left his business alone. As long as my music came first, I didn't care what he did.

But as time went on, Latif became very controlling. He started to see that my name alone was bringing out the crowds, and I no longer needed him to hold my hand. He was very wary when I would discuss business with others when he wasn't around. He felt like he had put money into me, so I belonged to him. I appreciated all that he had done, but I didn't want to be confined to a box. Musically I wanted to work with many other people, but if Latif didn't set it up then he wasn't down with it.

After opening a show for Shawty-Lo, I saw the hold that Latif had on my career get even tighter. I had been asked to go on tour with Lo and his team, and in the process, we became very close. He took me under his wing and laced me with game in the industry. He had been around before me, so he knew how it went. He didn't expect anything in return. He recognized my talents, and he wanted me to develop them. Although I was grateful for Lo's help, I could tell that Latif was uncomfortable with the new network I was creating on my own. And after I had started dating JC, one of Atlanta's hottest rapper at the time, Latif's insecurities began to cloud his vision. One night, after one of my performances, Latif pulled me to the side to question me about JC and my relationship. He started to see the time we were spending together was beginning to be more and more, and he felt like he was only trying to lead me away from his management company. We had built School House Productions together, and I had no desire to leave, but I couldn't convince Latif of that.

"You would be nobody without me. I put money into you. Not them," he said always wanting to remind me. But I didn't let that discourage me. I knew that Latif was under a lot of pressure. He was managing other artists outside of just me, he was having troubles in his marriage, and so every little thing sent him over the edge.

Three weeks into the tour, JC and I decided to call it quits. This made Latif extremely happy. I found out that he was married, and I was never going to be comfortable being the other woman. As much as I liked him, I knew, for the sake of my career, I had to let the situation go. This didn't stop Lo and my relationship though. We became thicker-than-thieves. Whenever he had a show, he would always let me perform. This bothered Latif because I was soon booking my own gigs, and he believed that I was only getting to perform as a way for Lo to get me to sign with his management company, but that was never the case. Between doing shows back-and-forth between home and Atlanta, I developed a crush on Lo's road manager Jay.

Jay was a little rough around the edges, but he was so sweet to me. He treated me like a queen so much so that all of the odds that were against him seem to be irrelevant. He had just gotten out of jail after doing six years, he was 28, and I was only 19, but he had been through a lot of the same things I had been through growing up. We connected on a level outside of music, outside of the physical, and Latif couldn't understand that. But I didn't care because Jay made me feel like the only girl in the world. If I wasn't flying out to see him, he was flying out to see me. I knew that if we got involved that it would a long-distance relationship, but he was worth it. I was willing to do whatever to make it work even if that meant lying to Latif.

It had been a few weeks since Jay and I began talking. Latif's suspicions continued, but I didn't let that stop me. During this time, I was on planes and in-and-out of hotel rooms just to keep our relationship a secret. I respected Latif as my manager, but my business was my business. And unfortunately, he didn't know how to separate the two. On one particular weekend, Jay was adamant that I be at one of Lo's shows. I never needed a reason to see them, so of course I agreed. Lo would let me perform, so I knew that my spot was set. Latif immediately had something to say. He felt like all business arrangements needed to go through him first, but Lo was family. We always had fun together, and that's what I loved the most.

After coming off stage from killing my performance, I noticed an altercation by the bar, and Lo was somehow right in the middle of it. As I approached the situation, the loud mouth girls arguing with him started to get even louder. One of the girls drunkenly spilled a drink right on Lo. Before she could say a word, he slapped fire across her face. Security hurried to get the girls out of the club. Lo was respected there, so their nonsense would not be tolerated. I quickly walked up to Jay wanting to know what happened as I looked out for Latif. He had been in the back counting the earnings from the night the last time I had seen him, and from the looks of the club, he hadn't moved.

"Baby, what happened?" I asked as security continued to usher the intoxicated groupies from the premises.

"Some girl fired off at the mouth saying Lo stepped on her shoe. He apologized, but it wasn't good enough for her."

The alcohol that continued to flow escalated the situation. These were the times I thanked God I didn't drink. I saw what it did to people especially after reading Denise's tox screen after she passed. I was good.

"You ready to go?" Jay asked tired of the dysfunction around us.

Being in a long-distance relationship was hard, so anytime that I had time to spend with him, I took advantage of it.

"Yeah, let me go tell Latif I'm going home."

"Okay, I'll be outside," Jay said grabbing Lo and the other fifteen people, they had come with.

I walked to the back office where Latif was still accounting for the money we had made that night. It was as if he was in a trance almost.

"Well, I'm bout to call it a night," I said interrupting.

"Naw, I needed to holla at you. This is yours," he said handing me my cut.

"Thank you," I said putting the stack of money into my purse.

"Now what were you saying?"

"I'm about to go home. The club is about to let out anyway."

"You need a ride?" he asked staring me up and down.

"No," I said wanting to avoid his gaze, "I drove. I'll talk to you tomorrow." I hurried out of the room before he could say anything else.

When I got outside, Jay was parked beside my car patiently waiting.

"You ready, baby?"

"Ready." I hopped into my car and followed behind him.

Ten minutes after Jay and I arrived at the hotel, Latif began calling my phone back-to-back. I ignored his calls throughout the rest of the night. I decided that whatever it was could wait until the morning, but Latif's persistence refused to let me sleep.

"Hello?"

"Where are you? I didn't see you leave the club."

"I told you that I was going home, remember?"

"Don't lie to me. I know you went with Jay back to his hotel room."

"What are you talking about?"

"I followed you, Skittlez," Latif admitted, "I took Greg's car, and you didn't even notice me following right behind you. You need to be more careful of your surroundings."

"Latif, you sound crazy. Are you drunk?" His paranoia was at an all-time high. Although I hid my relationship with J, I never wanted Latif to feel like he could tell who me who I could and could not date. He wasn't my father. I trusted him as my manager, but let him tell it, he made me.

"You must really think I'm stupid, huh? You don't think I know what's going on. All these back-and-forth trip aren't just for nothing, Skittlez. You're signing with Shawty Lo's team, huh? Tell me," he continued to yell into the phone, "They're just trying to take advantage of you, and you don't even see it. This is what you want to do?"

"Latif, I'm your artist. I am not your property. I'm not gonna apologize for spending time with my boyfriend while he's in town. It's hard enough being in a long-distance relationship without having to sneak around too."

"Skittlez, I'm gonna give you five minutes to come downstairs…"

I hung up the phone before he got the last word out. I put my phone on silent as the incessant calls continued. I refused to feel bad about mine and Jay's relationship anymore. Things were going really well, and for the first time, I could honestly say I was happy again. After that night, Latif and I were never the same. Soon my shows were cut shorter and shorter, and the money eventually dried up. He was being childish, and at that point, I decided that it would be best for both of us if we stopped working together. At first, I was convinced that he was the one who could help take me to the next level in my music, but he changed. And soon I began working with his assistant Amanda. She wasn't as well connected as Latif was, but I loved her drive. Amanda was able to give me the structure I was missing from working with Latif. He was upset that we had been working together, and that's when he assured me that the music came first, and he was ready to work.

During my junior year of college, I was asked to perform at an event in Phoenix, AZ. My aunt Cheryl lived in the city, so the trip sounded like a great opportunity. Latif arranged for me and my best friend Ashley to fly while he opted to drive. I didn't see why he wanted to take such a long route, but he said by driving, he would be able to bring our street team along with him. You can never receive too much promotion, so I was excited for them to join as well. Once we arrived in Phoenix, Cheryl picked us up from the airport. The show was in two days, so I decided to check in with Latif to make sure everything was still on schedule. He never answered. I didn't worry at first, but after Ashley and I got settled, he still wasn't answering the phone. I knew something was wrong. After being sent to voicemail for the last time, I decided to call Latif's wife Erica. She picked up on the first ring.

"Hello?"

"Hey, Erica, it's Skittlez. Do you know if Latif has his phone on him? I've been trying to call him all day."

"I mean he should. He hasn't even left yet," she said simply.

"What?" I asked in disbelief. It took at least thirty hours to get there, and we still had to rehearse. I knew that Latif would be cutting it close. "Can I talk to him please?" I was trying to keep my anger under control.

"What up?" Latif asked nonchalantly. His blatant disregard sent me over the edge.

"So when do you plan on leaving?"

"I don't."

"Excuse me?"

"Why don't you call 'ol boy?" he said smugly.

"Because you're my manager, Latif."

"Am I? Because you don't act like it. You constantly making moves without me. I know that Lo's team is trying to get you to sign with them. I'm not stupid."

"You know what? I can't do this anymore." I was done. I trusted Latif with my career, and he was willing to just throw it all away. After seeing that he would leave me unable to do a show, I knew that our contract couldn't be valid.

"I want out," I finally said. There was no more room for games.

"Good luck. We have a contract," Latif said laughing.

"Well, give me a copy, and I'll have my lawyer look over it."

"Lawyer? What lawyer?"

I was so young when I first signed with Latif. I should have known from the grammatical errors in the contract language that he wasn't as legit as he wanted to make it seem. There was no way that the contract was valid, but even if it was, I had called his bluff. I wanted out.

"I'm glad you got a lawyer. You're gonna need one," he said hanging up once he realized that his usual scare tactics had failed.

***

Life without Latif and School House Productions was hard in the beginning. After leaving, I began to work with Amanda on a more consistent basis. She wanted to get from under Latif's thumb as well, so our situation was a little less than ideal. Amanda didn't have the finances to back up her dreams of being a successful manager, and her network seemed to be smaller than mine. While she struggled to find a way, I began to grind again on my own. I went out and promoted my music to the different clubs around the city, but if Latif's name wasn't attached then the club owners didn't want to take the chance of not selling out. Despite the fact that I had sold out shows and clubs before too, they knew Latif always delivered. But after a few weeks, Amanda was able to get me in one of the hottest clubs in the city. I was ready to prove to everyone that my music spoke for itself, and I didn't need Latif to carry me. I built my fan base on the talents that God had given me and not Latif's name. During rehearsals that night, I noticed that he was backstage. We hadn't talked since he left me stranded in Phoenix, so I knew the interaction wouldn't be pleasant.

"What are you doing here?"

"I'm here to help," he lied.

"That's okay. I think me and Amanda have everything under control." I knew that he just wanted to see me fail, and I refused to give him the satisfaction.

"Look, Amanda filled me in on everything. Don't worry. I got this."

"Did my music get fixed?" Amanda had only one track, but I was doing a few songs that day, so I needed my music extended. It wasn't difficult to do, but I didn't trust Latif to do it right.

"Just go…" he insisted ignoring my previous question. With no time to waste, I took a deep breath as I prepared to take the stage. Once my music began to play, I relaxed. I was ready for the crowd.

My first number went as expected. My backup dancers floated around me as my lyrics rolled off my tongue. But suddenly, when we got ready to perform the next number, the music instantly stopped. I froze with a smile on my face praying the track continued, but it never did.

"Ya'll give it up for Mz. Skittlez," the club announcer shouted into the microphone as he ran across the stage. Embarrassed to say the least, I rushed backstage and immediately confronted Latif. The situation had his name written all over it.

"What happened to my music?" I yelled.

"I tried to tell you…"

"I can't believe that you would do something like this to me again. What is wrong with you?" Letting my anger get the best of me, I pushed him as hard as I could. He lost his balance almost falling off of the stage.

"Get out," he screamed.

"No problem." I grabbed my stuff quickly without having to be told twice. It was nothing but drama with Latif, and I was tired of it. I just wanted to do my music.

As I was walking out, I noticed that all of my dancers followed right behind me. They were tired of Latif's shady business practices too and refused to work for him any longer. That was the last straw. Many artists left the production company we had built together after that, and Latif was left with no one.

***

After one of the most embarrassing performances of my careers, I placed my focus back on school. Music would always be my first love, but I knew that I had other obligations as well. After being accepted to a study-abroad program, I began to prepare for two of the biggest moves of my life. For my senior year, I would be working and going to school in Atlanta for eight months and then New York for another eight months. I was excited for the opportunity. It was going to be nice to get a break from home and Latif's drama for at least a little while. And Jay and I had been doing the long-distance thing for a couple of months, so it was going to be good to be able to spend more time together. Rudy and Parker didn't want me to move so far, but they understood my desire to see new things. Although I had frequented the ATL a lot courtesy of Lo and Jay, I was excited to get my name out there.

After finalizing my plans for the move, I talked to one of my friends Michelle who already lived in Atlanta. She had a four-bedroom and had an empty room for rent. Luckily, I had gotten an internship at *Ozone Magazine*, so the rent wouldn't have been a problem, but I really didn't have any other choice. A few days before I was set to move in, Michelle and the other two girls were evicted. The rent hadn't been paid in months, and the owners finally had enough. I was devastated, but I had to act fast. Atlanta was happening whether I had a place or not, so I went on Roommate.com and met a girl who lived in the same area Michelle did. And come to find out, we had a mutual friend in common. I immediately called Tara to get information on my new roomie Samantha. Tara vouched for her, so with only her word to go on, I agreed to move in.

Jay and I didn't talk for the first couple of weeks after I arrived. I had been so distracted with finding a place and getting settled-in that the distance went temporarily unnoticed. But the more I called, the less he answered. The man I had spent hours with on the phone each night barely had enough time to say, "Hi." I felt like I was annoying him, but I needed to know something. Jay's disinterest was something I wasn't use to.

After a few more weeks passed, I finally got the call I had been hoping for.

"Hello?"

"Where have you been?" I asked.

"Look, I know that it seems like I've been ducking and dodging you lately, but that never was the case. I got into a little trouble…"

"Oh my gosh, what happened?" I asked as my tone changed, "Are you okay?" My defenses automatically went down. Jay and I basically had walked the same path. Our relationship was about more than what appeared on the outside. I saw myself in his reflection.

"I don't want to talk about it," Jay said quickly, "But I know you're out here now, and I can't wait to see you, but I just can't have you seeing me like this. It's not a good look. I'll be on house arrest for a little longer. I just need you to ride for me, okay?"

Stupidly, I ate up every last word. For almost eight whole months, I did not see Jay once. After that conversation, I spoke more to his voicemail than I ever did him. All the time we had spent together meant nothing. I then realized that Jay was only in our relationship out of convenience. Me living in Ohio gave him room to roam, but after I moved to Atlanta, I was too close to home. After realizing that our relationship would never be the same again, I returned my attention to work and school. I began performing again. And I knew that I could always depend on my godbrother Lo. Whenever he was doing a show, he would let me open as usual, so I was able to perform on a consistent basis as I continued to perfect my craft. Letting go of Jay was hard to do because I had put so much into us being together. But after not seeing each other for almost a year, I couldn't believe that I had moved all the way to Georgia in the first place. On my very last day in ATL, I had my U-Haul packed up and set for Cleveland. I would be going to New York for another eight months, but I needed to go home and get all of the winter clothes I had already packed for the trip. Before I could drive off, I received a call. It was Jay. I stared at my phone in confusion, as I hadn't seen his number in months. I tried to play it cool, but I was eager to see what he had to say for himself.

"What?" I snapped. I wanted him to hear my anger.

"I deserve that," he started, "How you been?"

"Oh you know just living in your city for almost a year now. Not that you care though."

"Listen, I know that how I went about the situation was wrong. I just didn't know how to be honest with you."

"About?"

Jay remained silent on the phone as he searched for the exact words to say.

"I wasn't completely honest about my relationship situation. I had a girl the whole time we were together. I just didn't know how to tell you. Don't get me wrong, I really digged you and everything, but you moving out here caught me off guard, and then I was put on house arrest. It was just really bad timing. I'm sorry though…"

I hung up the phone unable to listen to another word. All of the non-stop flights back-and-forth from Ohio to Georgia and late-night phone conversations were all lies. How could I have been so stupid? I tried to think back to remember if the signs that he was unfaithful had always been in front of my face, but there weren't any. Jay had been a perfect gentleman to me, and never in a million years would I have thought that there was anyone else. I didn't have time to dwell on the past, so I packed up my broken heart and headed back home to Cleveland. Next stop…New York.

10

"Don't tell people you dreams…show them."

Once I got back to Ohio, classes were right around the corner. After making sure that I had everything I needed for my move to New York, I moved back into the dorms to finish up a couple of things at school before I left. After everything that happened with Jay, I was done with guys. Every time I let someone get close to me, I was always the one getting hurt. But then there was always that one. Deyontay. A few days after being home, I got a text from a random number. I called the number back, and Deyontay immediately answered. I didn't really recognize his voice until he said my name. It had been so long.

"How you doing, Skittlez?"

"Deyontay?" Every few months he had a new number, so it was almost impossible to keep up with him. Despite all that we had been through, I still held a very special place for him in my heart. He was my first love after all.

"I heard you were back in town."

"Yeah, just for a little while though. I leave for New York in a couple of days."

"I wanna see you…"

"Why, Deyontay?" Some part of me wanted him, but I knew deep down that I had outgrown him. Continuing down the same dark path he had been on before, he remained in constant trouble. Over the few years we had been broken up, he was shot twice. I wanted to save him from himself. Obviously, God had him here for a reason, but he never found his purpose.

"It's been a while, Skittlez. Let me take you to dinner or something."

"I can't. I have my friend Ashley here with me."

"Bring her," he said simply.

"Bring her?"

"Yes. Look, I really wanna see you, man. Stop playing. You leaving for New York soon. Who knows the next time you'll be back."

"I'll be back," I said wanting to be difficult.

"Skittlez." I could tell I was testing his patience.

"Okay, hold on." I had to make sure that it was okay with Ashley first. Luckily, she didn't mind, so I accepted Deyontay's invitation.

About thirty minutes later, we arrived at his house. I parked in the driveway. Ashley and I decided to go inside for a few minutes. As we were walking up to the front door, empty beer bottles lined the grass and porch. It looked like a scene out of a bad frat house movie. As I carefully stepped through trash, Deyontay hurried to open the front door.

"Took ya'll long enough," he said smiling. He ran up to hug me with no other words spoken. His familiar smell comforted me. I had to admit a little piece of me missed him.

"Can I use the bathroom?" Ashley asked.

"Yeah, it's down the hall there on the right," he said pointing into the house, "Excuse the mess."

Trash covered the floor as if it was a garbage can. I knew that he wasn't the cleanliest person in the world, but the filth that surrounded him had gotten out of hand. After only a few minutes, I was ready to leave. Between Deyontay's random gun collection and smell that suffocated the house, I was just ready to get the night over with.

"Ya'll ready?" Deyontay asked grabbing his jacket, but before he walked outside, he slipped a .45 in the waist of his pants.

Immediately I stopped in my tracks. "What's that for?"

"Somebody might try and run up on me out here. You never know. I ain't about to be caught slipping though," he said patting his pants.

"Deyontay, seriously? Can you please leave it here?" I didn't need the drama.

"Skittlez, you heard what I said," he said walking out of the door.

"Well, I'm not going then. I'ma just go back home. I'm not about to be riding around with a gun in my car. Bye, Deyontay."

"Fine. Look," he said walking back into the house and leaving it on the table, "I'm leaving it here, okay? Can we go now?"

"Yes," I said with a smile on my face. I knew that he was a little rough around the edges, but he was just misguided. I wanted to help him; I had a bad habit.

As I let Deyontay lead the way, fifteen minutes later, I found myself in front of IHOP.

"This is dinner?" Ashley whispered into my ear as she got out of the car. All I could do was laugh. He tried, and that's all that mattered to me.

Once we were seated, Deyontay became even more belligerent. He began to harass the waitresses, as they would pass by our table.

"Ay, ya'll got any liquor up in here?" He just wanted to drink as me and Ashley shared an appetizer, but quickly, I lost my appetite.

He was unable to sit still, and I noticed that he kept fidgeting with his phone.

"Who's that?" I asked curious to know who had all of his attention. I mean he had asked me to dinner, but now he wasn't even paying me any mind.

"Damn, nosey. What you all up in mine for?" he snapped, "We ain't together."

"It was just a question. Chill."

"You ready, girl?" Ashley asked hoping to avoid the drama.

After Deyontay paid for our less than $20 'dinner', Ashley and I went back to the car. I could see the change in Deyontay, and I didn't like it. Every time I saw him, he seemed to get worse and worse.

"Take me to go get a black," he said hopping into the car.

"No." Mind you we had to stop prior to even getting to IHOP. "Why didn't you get two when you were at the store?"

"You know what? I'm done with you," he yelled. I had never seen him so angry before in my life. It was as if he became another person—a person I didn't know. "You think you're better than me, huh?"

"Deyontay, what are you even talking about? I'll take you to the store, okay?" He was scaring me, and I just didn't want to fight.

As I was driving back to his house, he kept turning the music all the way up, and he was jumping around in his seat. He banged his fist against his chest and said a few words that I couldn't make out.

"What you say?" I asked turning down the volume.

"I said when I get out of this car, I'm shooting it up. I would do it right now if I hadn't listened to you earlier."

"Deyontay, please don't play like that," Ashley said wanting to diffuse the situation.

"You think I'm playing?" he asked with all seriousness.

By this time, I began to get nervous. He had fired a gun right above my head while we were still dating, so I knew how reckless he could be. He promised that it was by accident, but I knew better. Not knowing who else to call, I called my dad hoping that he would be able to talk some sense into him.

"Hello?"

"Dad? Listen, I went to dinner with Deyontay, and now he's saying that he is going to shoot my car up."

"What?" he yelled out in confusion, "What do you mean he said he's gonna shoot the car up?"

"Exactly what I said. I'm just trying to drop him off."

"Mary, why would you even be around him? You're leaving in a couple days, so now you decide to hang out with him of all people. You know he's crazy. Let me talk to him." Art was disappointed to say the least. He had never liked Deyontay while were together even though Deyontay had the utmost respect for him. My dad could sense that something was wrong with him, but I was never able to see it until that moment.

"It's my dad," I said slowly handing Deyontay my phone.

"Listen, I have a lot of respect for you, sir, but your daughter is out of pocket. She thinks that she's better than me just because she's going to New York. I'ma show her who's better than who," he said hanging up the phone. He made a gun with his fingers and jammed them into the side of my forehead.

Deyontay let his anger consume him as we drove back to his house. The constant ringing of his phone didn't help the situation either.

"Why are you calling me?" he barked into the phone.

"Cause I'm outside," I heard a female voice say.

"But I told you I was busy. If you're still at my house when I get there, it's gone be a problem."

Mz. Skittlez

I was thankful for the distraction. I hoped that this new girl would make Deyontay forget his idle threats. I was wrong. When I pulled up to his house, the girl on the phone was still sitting on the porch waiting. As soon as she saw him, she got up and began to walk over to the car.

"You better go. Your little friend is…" Before I could finish my sentence, Deyontay punched me in the side of the head as he quickly got out of the car. The girl stopped walking when she saw him run up to his front door with me not that far behind.

I had grown up with all brothers, so I had taken a beaten or two before, but there was no way that I was going to allow a man to put his hands on me. First love or not. Feeling the adrenaline course through my veins, Deyontay squared up with me like I was another man. We fought in the middle of his yard with no regard for those around us. I had a point to prove.

As I gave him a jab to the mouth, he pushed me down and ran into the house.

"Let's go," Ashley yelled. She had spent the entire fight trying to break us up, but there was no use.

Deyontay's friend stood on the sideline as if she was watching a Pay-Per-View event until she saw him come outside with a gun in his hand. I didn't really think that he would ever hurt me, so I knew he wasn't going to shoot me.

"Let's go, Skittlez," Ashley continued to yell.

After seeing the pure hatred in his eyes, I realized that he was serious. As Ashley quickly drove off, Deyontay pointed the gun straight at me. The bullet didn't hit the car, but the shot was too close for comfort, and I knew that at that moment, any love that I had for him died. The next day, Deyontay called every few minutes, texted me, and left me voicemails saying that he didn't want to lose me. After all that, I believed his cries for forgiveness. He went on-and-on about how he wasn't himself, and he didn't remember what happened. He had been battling bipolar disorder and manic depression, but he always swept it under the rug. He needed help, but he was too proud to ask for it. As much as I loved him, I couldn't sacrifice myself in the process. Deyontay's outbursts became more frequent and more violent as the years went on. I knew that it was only a matter of time before he hurt himself or someone else. But that someone could not be me. That same day, I blocked my number, and I have never spoken to Deyontay Binds again.

***

Ending things with Deyontae once and for all was the thing I needed to do most. We had held onto to each other for so long out of comfort that neither one of us knew how to let go, but the time had come. New York was going to be a new chapter for me, and I didn't want to waste it by crying over spilled milk. Deyontay and Jay were now in my past, and I was ready for the future.

In their usual godparent fashion, Rudy and Parker helped me move into my first apartment in New York. I lived right off of 30th and 8th in Manhattan. It was directly across the street from Madison Square Garden. From first glance, I felt at home despite the super small apartment. With just 900 sq. ft., I only had room for my clothes and bed, so I learned how to downsize. Rudy was in tears again about me being so far from home, but I assured them that I would be fine. Ashley and I had moved out there together, so I felt better knowing I wouldn't have to be alone. The apartment was fully furnished, so I was able to tuck away the money I made from working at FruityLoops as well as my side styling jobs for many celebrities in Atlanta. But soon I realized my savings would only pay for my basic needs, so my music had to take a back seat. New York was huge, so I knew that I had to start creating opportunities for myself. I would book time at famous studios throughout the city. I just wanted my music to be heard. Whether I was in the booth, or out in the hallway writing, I wanted to make as many contacts as I could. This habit of mine became expensive quickly, and the money I had saved up wasn't enough for my rent, bills, and music costs. In an attempt to get my name out there without so much strain on my wallet, I performed at any open-mic I could find, but I quickly realized that there were vast amounts of girls who looked just like me, and sounded just like me. Everything that had set me apart in Cleveland was the norm in New York. My wild and colorful attire was strongly celebrated as I frequented the streets of the city. Despite feeling accepted, I felt overshadowed. I had built such as strong fan base in Cleveland and Atlanta that I assumed the same thing would happen there too, but I was wrong. I was out of my element, and I didn't want my music to suffer. I knew that it was going to be hard, but I was determined to make it.

Rudy and Parker were willing to help me, but I didn't feel right taking money from them anymore. While in her third grade year, Rudy enrolled Apples in a private school in the area, and the tuition alone was very high. They had been providing greatly for her while allowing me to finish school, so that I could provide a better life for the both of us.

I knew that I couldn't ask Diane for anything, and Art made it more than clear that I was on my own. He didn't understand me wanting to move all the way to New York anyway.

"If you do this, Mary, you do this on your own." His words echoed throughout my head. There was only one thing I had to do. I had to get a job.

***

I started out as a studio receptionist, but working there was not in my best interest. I continued to do side jobs such as acting and modeling just to keep my name relevant, but nothing seem to be working out. I was lost. Then one day, I went into Topshop. From the moment I walked in, I fell in love. From the décor to the fashion, it was everything that I embodied. As I browsed around the store, the sales girl on the floor quickly greeted me.

"O.M.G., I love your style. Where'd you get it?" she asked pointing to my outfit.

"I actually designed it myself," I said proudly.

"That is amazing. You know what? You should really work here. I think you'd be perfect. I'm Christina by the way," she said smiling.

"Nice to meet you, Christina, I'm Skittlez."

"Of course you are. That's so fun. Now listen, Skittlez, we're having interviews all day tomorrow. And just from your style, I can tell that you would be a great addition to the team. Please tell me you'll come."

I didn't really have a choice, so I filled out an application and had a group interview the very next day. It consisted of different challenges from basically everything I had been learning in school plus the few styling jobs I had done. I was more than ready. I passed each

The Icing On Top Ain't Always Sweet

test with flying colors to say the least, and Topshop's management took notice. I was hired there on the spot.

"What's a good salary for you?" It was a good question that I had never been asked before. "$1,000,000 an hour," I wanted to say, but I knew that they were looking for something more realistic.

"Is $17 okay?" I asked unknowingly underselling myself. Later I found out that the guy's position I took was making $24 an hour, but by the end of things, I received $21, and I wasn't going to complain.

During an interview, one of the first questions was about our prior styling experience. "Do you have a clientele base?" a woman on the panel asked.

All of my clients were in Atlanta, so I embellished a little to begin with because I knew they were trying to get as many celebrities into the doors as possible. After the interview, I shadowed one of the store's employees Jorge. He was so fun to be around. His flamboyant personality blended so well with mine. As we took a tour throughout the store, we found ourselves riding down in the elevator singing Miley Cyrus' "Party in the USA" with every floor that passed. Our voices echoed throughout the small, metal box, and when the elevator reached the ground floor, we were face-to-face with one of Disney's biggest female stars.

"Nice song," she said smiling, "I love your style. Come with me." I couldn't believe that I was meeting someone so famous, and I hadn't even started the job yet. I knew that Topshop was the right move.

As we followed Ms. Disney herself, I knew that we would not deal with her directly. She was the artist, but she was more down to earth than I could have ever imagined. Ms. Disney continued to admire the small cupcake tattooed on my leg, as we talked about my passions for the small, delicious treats. This led the conversation to the clothing line that I wanted to develop. After that, her publicist Sarah gave me her contact information and encouraged me to keep in touch. I was excited by the new connection, and I knew that I was finally on the right path. And while working at Topshop, I was able to exercise my styling skills as I created different looks for many A-list celebrities. One invaluable thing that I learned while styling and pursuing my music was that relationships are the most important thing you can have in the entertainment industry. I can credit my success to my personality, but also to the relationships, I was able to develop and nurture. They were something I could use no matter where I was. I finally realized that my network equaled my net worth.

***

  While working at Topshop, I gained so much experience, but I still wasn't making enough to support my musical endeavors. And going to open-mics every night didn't have my music where I needed it to be. I had to switch it up. So after finding an ad on Craig's List for a venue, I decided that I could host my own open-mic. I had been to so many throughout my time in New York that I had the process down. For eight months, Ashley and I booked the venue every Friday for $350. We charged admission to get in and a fee to perform. Soon we were making more money than we knew what to do with. I would usually open each show, and the artists who signed up to perform would follow. Although I enjoyed my time on stage, I was performing archived music. I promised myself that when I got back home, I was going to spend my time writing new material. I had gone through so much over the last couple of years that the lyrics sat on my soul. It was time.

  Graduation was quickly approaching, but I wasn't ready to leave New York. Kent State wouldn't allow me to walk the stage at the extension school I attended, so I had no choice but to go back home. A part of me was torn. While trying to get over my break-up with Jay, I started dating Dre, a security guard at a boutique I frequented. He was the sweetest guy I had ever met, and that sweetness definitely grew on me. He knew that I was only going to be in the city for eight months, so we tried to make the best of things. I loved spending time with him because his story was so similar to my own. He had a rough childhood, and he was the first person in his family to graduate from college. Dre and I would talk for hours. I loved how his personality was so laid back. I appreciated that he didn't have that natural New York aggression, but seven months into our relationship, I realized that I was using him to get over Jay. I was still hurt even though I couldn't admit it. A few weeks before I was set to go back home, Dre became very distant. We talked about having a long distance relationship in the

The Icing On Top Ain't Always Sweet

beginning, but as the time for me to leave got closer, he had a change of heart.

In 2009, I moved back to Cleveland right before Christmas. While at home, I hit the pavement hard and put 100% of my time into my music. I later found out that an uncle of mine who had recently passed left his house in my name. This was blessing directly from God. Soon after that, I moved from the dorms into my new house and reconnected with my prior manager Amanda. I always loved working with her, and she had stepped her game up from the last time we worked together. Between performing and radio and television interviews, I did my best to continue to get my name out there. I became so busy with work that Dre and my relationship suffered. I had later learned that he was upset by me moving back to Cleveland even though he knew my arrangement from day one. He made sure that he had a plan B, but I was never going to be okay with being an option, so I decided to call it quits. I was used to being hurt, so I let the ending of our relationship be the fire I needed to finally move on.

***

In January of that next year, I had a show coming up, and I needed to get all of the costumes secured. I had mostly everything for the performance except for my back-up dancers' shoes. With no time to waste, I opted for a small, Indian owned shoe store in the area. I found the exact shoes I was looking for with no problem at all, but after dropping them off to the girls; one of them called back and said that her pair was the wrong size. They didn't fit. We didn't have time to go out and find new shoes, so I urged her to hurry and try to exchange them for the correct size. A few hours later, Crystal called again and said that they had her size, but they wouldn't do the exchange without the original sales receipt. My premature sigh of relief quickly went away. I had the receipt in my pocket. Here I was on the other side of town, and the store was about to close. I didn't know how I was going to make it, but I had to try. Fifteen minutes later, I ran into the store with the small white piece of paper in hand.

"Thank you so much for this," I said a little out of breath.

"Hey, I know you…" the Pakistani salesman continued to say with a wide grin from ear-to-ear. I assumed that he had seen my face from around town somewhere because there was no way that he listened to my music. The owners and sales associates were very traditional.

"Can I ask you a favor?" he asked in his thick accent, "My nephew likes you. You two should go on date." I was thankful that we were able to get everything we needed for the performance, so I agreed just to be nice.

"Sure."

As the salesman was putting Crystal's shoes in a bag, Zahid, his nephew slowly approached me.

"How are you?" he asked nervously. He barely looked me in the eyes.

"I'm fine. Nice to meet you, I'm Mary."

"So it's okay to take you on date?" he asked.

"Yes, I would love to. What did you have in mind?"

"Dinner? Movies?"

"That sounds great. I'll come pick you up tomorrow night."

Zahid was different from any other guy I had been with. He had only been in the country for four years, so his English was not very good, but I didn't mind. Initially I saw it as another networking opportunity, so I embraced the culture shock. During our first date, many things were lost in translation. I quickly realized that Zahid was not Americanized at all, and I was having trouble explaining every little thing to him. While we watched *Death at a Funeral*, I could tell that he wasn't getting the jokes. He watched me the whole time as he mimicked my expressions. Whenever I laughed, he laughed, but his timing was always a little off. But as time went on, we began spending more and more time together. I loved being around him because everything was so new to him. I was able to see the simplest things perceived through new eyes. Zahid was a breath of fresh air. He didn't try to be anyone other than himself. He constantly wore traditional dishdashas and sandals no matter what the weather was like. My personality was the complete opposite. While Zahid preferred simplicity, my colorful attire intrigued him.

The more time we spent together, the more I liked him. His work ethic mirrored my own. He wanted to prove to his manager that he could own his own store too one day. I encouraged him to follow his dreams, but the mom-and-pop shop he worked for was good enough for him at the time. I thought that I was a usually shy person, but it took Zahid a while to come out of his shell. He had never had a girlfriend before, so he didn't know how to interact with me. He was always so nervous. Back in his country of Pakistan, he had an arrangement set up between his parents and the parents of a mystery girl, but he went against tradition. He didn't want to be forced into marriage; he wanted to find true love. He was a blank canvas that I was able to paint as I pleased. I thought that I had created the perfect man. I could tell that his feelings were developing for me too. I had to teach him everything from how to dress to even how to use a knife and fork. He was so appreciative of the effort I put into him. I took him from nothing, but no one around the city believed that we were really an item. Zahid was a very simple man.

    He was never flashy; it wasn't in his blood. He only had enough money to survive. Rumors started to fly around the city, and people would say that he was only with me to receive his green card, but that wasn't the case. Zahid already had his green card when we met. He didn't have a car. He lived at home with his father, stepmother, and younger siblings. He didn't have anything, but he was so sweet that none of that mattered to me. And even though our relationship continued to blossom, his family was not pleased. His father hated all of the time we were spending together. He made is a point to tell family members back home that Zahid was in a relationship with a black stripper. After seeing my colorful personality, the color of my skin, and my music videos, his father was convinced that I was wrong for his son, but my family on the other hand loved him.

    A few months into our relationship, I was offered to go on tour for four weeks with Ms. Disney, the Disney channel star I had met on my first day at Topshop. Cheryl had run into her publicist Sarah in Phoenix. A little while after our initial meeting, Sarah and I had lunch a few times. I kept in touch with her via email, so I knew that the opportunity to go on tour was a sign that I had to take. This was around the same time I graduated college at Kent State University. My graduation was perfect. All of my family, even my mother Diane, were able to come together to celebrate one of the most important days of my life with me. Zahid and I had been together for a few months by this time. He was unable to make the ceremony because he had to work that day, but I understood. His drive and ambition to be successful in this country was just as strong as mine was, and it was one of the things that I loved about him. Excited about the new career opportunity, I began to get ready for the month long trip until my aunt Cheryl brought me back down to reality. Although I was added to the ticket, getting there was going to be expensive. As a fresh college graduate, I was strapped for cash, but I was determined to see my name in lights, so I pleaded with my friends and family. If no one understood, I knew they would. My family had seen how hard I worked, and they would do anything to help me pursue my dreams. I let them all know that I didn't want any gifts for my graduation present. The only thing I needed was money. After rallying together, my family contributed $1,000 to my trip, and Zahid took care of the rest. I was so thankful. I had the $1,500 I needed to book my first flight over seas.

 The tour was everything I thought it would be and more. For the first time in my music career, I felt like all of my hard work was finally being acknowledged. The tour was paying me $1,500 a day. I was used to performing for free, so the new money flow was unexpected. As I continued to collect the checks, I honestly didn't know what they were for. I didn't open any others after the first one. I just knew there had to be some sort of mistake. I called the tour manager hoping to rectify the situation. Things were going great, and I didn't want to ruin it by knowingly being over paid.

 When I spoke to Melissa, she said, "I added you to the write-up. Didn't you know?"

 It was news to me, but I was thankful nonetheless. After a few weeks into the tour, it was cut short, but I had made another $15,000 in addition to the money I had been putting up. To be fresh out of college and have $20,000 in cash would be anyone's dream. I was so excited to come home. I kept a list of the things I wanted to buy when I arrived back in Cleveland. First thing was my all pink Range Rover. I was home only a few hours before my dad took me to the dealership to buy my dream car. The money I held in my purse was burning a hole through it. I couldn't spend it fast enough. I knew exactly what I wanted, and the car dealer was more than happy to oblige, but I couldn't shake the judgment I felt from my dad as we sat in the show room.

"What are we doing here?" he asked impatiently.

"What do you mean?" I asked excitedly looking over the purchase contract.

"You haven't even paid off your student loans yet. I understand you want a new car, but is all this necessary?"

"Yes." Or at least I wanted it to be.

"What do you really want to do?" he asked me not convinced.

I sat back in the plush leather seat and twirled the pen I was about to sign the contract with around my fingers. I had an idea, but I didn't know if it could become reality, but I was willing to give it a shot. What did I have to lose?

"I want my own clothing line."

11

"Sometimes the person who you would take a bullet for is the one behind the gun."

After realizing that I had as big of a passion for fashion as I did for music, I decided to go for it. I graduated with a degree in Fashion Merchandising, with a double minor in Business Management, and Marketing, and I knew that I needed to start using them, so I reached out to the owner of Donnard's a popular clothing store in the area. After speaking with Donnard, I tried to convince him that we should go into the business together. I wanted to be his partner, but he had other ideas.

"I would rather you be a visual merchandiser or a buyer. Something like that."

I understood his concern. I was young with not a lot of prior experience, but I had the drive to become successful at whatever I put my mind to. I really didn't have any other choice, so I accepted Donnard's offer to be the store's buyer but only as a challenge. What I lacked in experience, I made up for in vision. I knew what I wanted, and there was nothing that was going to stand in between me and securing that partnership. Two weeks later, Donnard was finally convinced. As soon as my feet hit the door, I worked harder than everyone else there. I was always the first one in and last one to leave at night. I was on a mission, but my relationship suffered because of it. After a few weeks of working at Donnard's, Zahid became very controlling. He couldn't understand that fact that I was so busy. Although it was unintentional, he felt like I wasn't making enough time for him. I just saw it as a small sacrifice, but that wasn't good enough. He wanted me around all the time, but that time, I didn't have. My feelings for Zahid began to grow stronger each day despite his controlling behavior, and I began to second-guess if I was making the right decision by pursuing my career, or if I was just thinking about myself.

Very suddenly, Zahid experienced a death in his family. I wanted to be there to support him, but time did not allow it, so he traveled back to Pakistan with his family to deal with their lost. I promised that when he got back that things were going to change for the better. We had been in such a rocky place after I graduated that I was willing to do anything to make it better, but as time went on, things only got worse. When Zahid returned back to the states, he was even more persistent about us spending more time together, but his possessive nature made me want to do the opposite. His pressures and expectations of me were too much. Our relationship became a chore for me, and I think he could tell. Out of spite for my lack of attention, Zahid suddenly had girls all throughout his phone. Inappropriate messages filled his inbox from females who were just showing interest because we were together. By this point, I really cared about him. I knew that his outbursts were just a cry for my attention, so I decided that I would give it all up just to make him happy.

"If you think I'm cheating on you, I'll quit," I used to tell him over and over again. He would never let me.

But after losing his job at the store, Zahid found that he had nothing but time on his hands, and I found myself busier than ever. Deep down, I always felt like he resented me for it. All of our dates stopped, and I was put in a position to take care of everything financially. Zahid never had a lot of money to begin with, but he tried. After he was fired, our relationship was never the same again. He lost a piece of his manhood. As the months went on, I found myself losing focus on us. I wasn't happy anymore. As much as I loved him, all of his insecurities were hard to deal with. And with Ashley moving to Akron, I had no one to talk to. I began to bury myself in my work again making it even harder for Zahid and me. When he saw that I wasn't slowing down, and more of my time was being consumed at Donnard's, he knew that he had to do something. After receiving a call from his brother in Pakistan, Zahid went back home to work at his family's business. I hated to see him leave, but I knew that it was for the best. He said that he was only going to be gone for a month, but this was the break we needed. I would be able to work without judgment, and he would be able to regain his confidence while making the money we needed. After a year and a half of being together, it hurt me to see him so unhappy, but I felt the same way. Something had to change.

While Zahid was away, I continued to work long hours at Donnard's, but even from across the world, his insecurities continued. If I didn't answer the phone quickly enough, he was convinced that I was being unfaithful even though I was determined to prove my love to him. But as one month became two, my family was convinced that he left me and was never coming back, and after a while, their words began to resonate. *What if he doesn't come back?* I would ask myself, *Where does that leave me?* My mind was playing tricks on me. I didn't know what to believe.

Zahid hoped that our daily Skype calls would keep us strong, but they only made me feel worse. The entire time he would question my whereabouts and who I had been around. His jealousy was much more apparent. It was exhausting that I was faithful to him and always had been, but that wasn't good enough for him. He would bring up my location and names of people I had been talking to on the phone or texting. I was convinced that he was stalking me, but it seemed almost impossible since he was all the way in Pakistan, so I tried to let it go. The long distance put more of a strain on us than ever before, but Zahid was beginning to put in more of an effort. His constant accusations of me cheating on him finally stopped. I was able to breathe a little, so I returned my attention to Donnard's

A few weeks later, a friend of mine texted me and asked, *Have you been on Twitter?*

I hadn't been on it that day, so I immediately replied, *No*, but my curiosity got the best of me, so I logged in. I soon realized that all of my pictures had been deleted, and fake naked pictures with my head attached had been posted in their place. I was shocked by the hate that was spewed on my page. Whoever did it had it in for me, but I just couldn't imagine who. My first instinct was to call the police. My rights had been violated, and I wanted whoever was responsible to pay for what they did. The police tried to get me to list the people who could have possibly done it, and for some reason my mind kept going back to Zahid. I tried to shake the thought, but I couldn't. A few days before, he called me and asked for the password to where I kept my music, which was the same one I used for my Twitter account. He said that he wanted to let his friends listen to my mixtape. I never thought twice about it, but I should have known that he had something to do with it. More and more, he would ask about people he had never even met before, or he would know where I had been at any given time. At first, I thought that I was being followed, but later I found out that he had been tracking my every move from Pakistan. While away, he had been working for the Sprint of the country and had access to all of their phone records and minutes, so he and his brother had been tracking my location and every conversation that I had. I couldn't believe that the man I was in love with would intentionally try and hurt me. He promised that he was going to work on trusting me, but this stunt proved that he went back on his word. Once I put two-and-two together, I immediately called Zahid. Of course, he denied it with every part of his being, but I could tell he was lying. And as usual, he tried to turn the situation around on me.

"I can't believe you would think I would do something like this to you," he said in his thick accent. But he gave me no reason to think otherwise.

After the Twitter fiasco, I was done with my relationship with Zahid for the time being. He didn't trust me, and he made me feel guilty about every little thing. I couldn't take it anymore. I needed space, but Zahid refused to let me go. He called me every day and left voicemails trying to convince me that he loved me and would never do anything to hurt me. He went on Twitter and tried to stand up for me in the mist of the embarrassing situation. He wanted to prove that he was on my side. He stuck to his story, and eventually, I began to believe in his words. After a while, he finally admitted that he had been spying on me in fear of losing us, but he promised that he would work on trusting me. I wanted to believe him, so I forgave him and gave him a second chance. Things began to get a little better as the weeks passed, but I still wasn't happy. What was supposed to be a one-month trip quickly turned into six. We weren't in a good place, but I had invested two years into Zahid, and I didn't know if I was ready to let it all go.

After opening an investigation on my Twitter account being hacked into, the FBI shut it down. The story had gotten out, and it was on the radio and in the news, but soon it blew over. I thanked God that no damage had been done. I was ready to put it all behind me. But even after all that, the trouble continued. A month later, Zahid had gotten in trouble and had to come home. He was detained in Pakistan for not paying his taxes. He had to pay $9,000, but the police would keep coming back to collect every day. And if he didn't pay, they threatened to take him to jail, so he came back to the states. Despite all that happened between, I was excited for him to come back. With Zahid being in another country, it made it hard for our relationship, but I knew that with him being home, we would be able to reconnect again, or at least I hoped we would.

When he finally arrived home, it was a few weeks before my birthday, and all I wanted was a new car. After my dad had convinced me not to buy my dream car, I settled for the car I had. But after Zahid returned, he said that he would go half with me. I felt a little better knowing that the financial burden of our relationship was not solely on me anymore. Zahid was able to contribute again, and this time, he was ready to take the next step. With marriage being a topic that came up frequently, Zahid thought that it was time we moved in together. I was all for the idea because it was hard to have to sneak into his father's house every time I wanted to see him. We looked at a few places, but we both fell in love with a condo that was in the area. I was thrilled to have him all to myself. I knew that it would be the perfect time to work on rebuilding our relationship, but my dreams quickly came to an end when I found out that his older brother was coming to live with us as well. In their culture, the brother was the king. And being that their father left Pakistan to move to America, Zahid's brother had to accept the role as the man of the house at a very early age. After we moved in, all of his siblings made themselves right at home. His sisters would come from their father's house to cook and clean and to make sure that I was taking proper care of their brother. They wanted to shape me into the perfect wife for Zahid. Even though we weren't married, he lied to his family and said we were. It was against tradition for a man and a woman to live together out of wedlock, so I played the role as the adoring wife. I changed everything about myself in hopes of making everyone happy. I tried to meet Zahid's family's expectations in hopes that I could be the woman they all wanted me.

As Zahid and I continued to live in pretend matrimony, his controlling ways and insecurities became even worse. He was convinced that I was unfaithful and had been throughout our entire relationship, but he was wrong. In fear that I would leave him, he made me promise that I would no longer have contact with any men I had prior relationships with, platonic or otherwise. He was paranoid about the past and the crazy reality he had created for himself. As time went on, I found myself feeling stuck. I wanted out, but that wasn't an option for Zahid.

One night while we were watching TV, he asked, "What store is open late that sells jewelry?" It was almost midnight.

"Walmart sells jewelry, I think," I said without thinking twice.

"Put on some clothes," he said jumping off the couch like it was on fire.

Thirty minutes later, I found myself in a deserted Walmart in the middle of the night. Zahid was adamant about getting me a band. We looked around for a few minutes before he finally settled on a small gold ring. It couldn't have been more than $100, but Zahid saw it as a promise that we would be husband and wife. I thought that the gesture was sweet, but again I didn't think we were going to get married anytime soon. I was young, and honestly, marriage was the last thing on my mind. A few days later, Zahid woke me up out of my sleep and said that we had to get married that week.

"Why do you wanna get married so fast?" I asked with sleep still in my eyes, but I already knew the answer. I had to conform to his family's traditions.

"You can have the 'happily-ever-after,' or you can move back home. I'll give you the money back for the condo."

I was speechless. I didn't want to lose him, but I didn't know if I was ready to be married yet. Things still weren't right between us, so I didn't think a quick fix was what we really needed. But without protest, Zahid gave me the date he had already set for that week. He had organized everything by himself. The night before we got married, I had a vivid nightmare that I can still remember to this day. My family disowned me because they were so disappointed that I agreed to the shotgun wedding in the first place. I knew that they wanted to be a part of a more traditional wedding where I had a beautiful white dress, and with my father giving me away, but that's not how Zahid saw it. On the day of the wedding, we went to the courthouse, got married, and then went out to breakfast shortly after. I had to go to work, so the celebration was cut short. Even after that there was no honeymoon; things returned to how they always had been.

I thought that by us finally being husband and wife that I would feel closer to Zahid and his family, but for some reason, I felt even more isolated than before. Coming home to a family that wasn't mine every night made me feel alone. Their culture was different, and they refused to speak anything other than Urdu when they were all together. I ended up learning a few words and phrases, but I still couldn't relate to them. Apples would come over almost every weekend, so I had a little piece of home, but during the rest of the week, I felt like an outsider. I was in a different atmosphere. Zahid's brother and sisters made me feel welcomed to the best of their abilities. They would encourage me to learn how to cook different foods from their homeland and would insist that we cooked together as a family, but it was hard for me to maintain my responsibilities at work and all the ones at home too. When I would get off, the whole family would be waiting for my return. In their culture, they could not eat until every member of the house was present. So as soon as I stepped foot inside the door, Zahid's sister would begin to fix dinner no matter how late it was. They would run around the kitchen heating up the food they had happily prepared while they sang songs in their language. I felt like I was putting on an act that I couldn't keep up with.

Once dinner was complete, Zahid or his brother would take their sisters home, but then it would time for Zahid and me to spend time together. This daily routine was hard to keep up with. I was exhausted. I didn't have the time to work all day, come home late, have an authentic but very heavy Pakistani meal, and then tend to Zahid's needs as well. I soon became burnt out. During this time, I realized that we were wrong for each other. His expectations of me became too much, and I unknowingly began to resent him. I knew that our marriage was not going to work, but I prayed to God each night to make me fall back in love with Zahid, but it never happened. I tried to cover up my unhappiness with materialistic things. I would tell myself that we would have beautiful children together, or that we lived in such a nice place, and we both drove nice cars, but I realized that I was only focused on these things to cover up the fact that I was miserable, but no matter what, these things could never overshadow his many insecurities.

One day after talking to an old friend on Twitter, Zahid came home furious. I never took his threat of me not talking to other people seriously. I was willing to do a lot for him and our relationship, but I was never willing to let him dictate who I spoke to.

"You said that you were gonna be faithful," he continued to yell, "Why did you have to message him?" He wouldn't allow me to get word in.

I quickly realized that he was still stalking me and tracking my whereabouts and conversations even though he had promised that it was all behind us. Nothing I did or said would calm him down, so I called my dad hoping that he would be able to talk some sense into him. When Zahid got on the phone, he tried to convince my dad that I was the one in the wrong.

"She's not a real wife," he blurted out, "She doesn't even know how to cook."

My father wasted his breath, as there was no convincing Zahid. He threw my phone down and rushed into the bedroom we shared. With all of his strength, he pulled my clothes down breaking all of the hangers in the process and threw them into a pile in the middle of the room along with my shoes. I begged him to stop, but my cries fell on deaf ears. He became so aggressive that he scared me. I had no other choice but to call the police. As I grabbed my phone to call, he snatched it from me and threw it into the wall making it stick into the plaster. Zahid's brother rushed into the room after hearing all of the commotion and ran to comfort me.

"What is wrong with you, Zahid?" he yelled. At this time, I appreciated his concern, but I later found out that he was only worried about Zahid receiving an American passport, so he couldn't let him get into trouble. "Let her get her stuff and leave."

Confused and with tears clouding my vision, I grabbed as much of my stuff as I could and packed it all in my truck. I was having the house my uncle left me renovated, but until everything was settled between me and Zahid, it would be home. For a few weeks, I took a time out and reevaluated what we were really doing in our relationship. I didn't know if I should've put any more effort or just finally let it go.

In my heart, I wanted out. Zahid's conscience was constantly playing games on him. No matter how much I tried to prove that I loved him, or how much time we spent together, he was convinced that I was nothing but a cheater, someone who was incapable of being faithful. And soon enough became enough.

"I want a divorce," I said simply one day. I knew that he would freak, but it was time to address the elephant in the room.

"What did you say?" Zahid asked confused as if I was speaking a foreign language. Well, I guess to him, I was.

"You heard me, Zahid," I said quietly.

"If you want a divorce, you won't get a dime from me. You know that, right?" Zahid's brother started a business back in Pakistan that allowed him to bring his family out of poverty. What started out as only an idea, later became a multi-million dollar business. Zahid wanted me to depend on his family's money, but it wasn't worth it. After being controlled and verbally and mentally abused for three years, there was no amount of money that would have made me stay.

"Keep your money, Zahid. I just want my life back."

"I love you. Why can't you just be happy with me?" he yelled, "You made me. Why would you build a plane from the ground up just to let the next girl fly first class?"

"Because I got tired of the pilot."

I didn't say another word as I walked out of the door.

12

"My future is a present..."

After Zahid and I separated, Cleveland was never the same for me. Even though we were no longer together, people would always come up to me to report his every move, but I knew that his bad behavior was a cry for attention, and I chose to ignore it. I had success with the store and the beginning stages of branding Cupcake Mafia, but there was still so much to do. While Zahid was out of the country, I started Cupcake Mafia with only $300. This was enough for only thirty shirts. At that time, $300 was a lot to just throw down the drain, but I believed in my dream. It had to work. Originally, Cupcake Mafia was created by me and two of my friends, Keke and Stacey, to bring females artists together. It was more of a networking opportunity, but I had wanted to start my own clothing line for the longest, and the name was perfect. When I went to Keke and Stacey about the idea, they immediately lost their enthusiasm for the project. $100 apiece was all it was going to take, but they weren't interested in investing any money at all. They just wanted to make a quick buck. I was frustrated by their lack of work ethic, but I was determined to keep going. And one of my other friends D saw my hard work and wanted to invest in my dream.

"You're a walking billboard," he said giving me $150 just because he had faith in my talents. After that, I started doing research day-and-night. I was able to hook up with one of the printers in the area, and I also found a designer to create the Cupcake Mafia logo, and from that day, my business was born.

Even though Keke and Stacey didn't believe in the brand, I still tried to keep them involved, but that meant that every expense came directly from my own pocket. I paid for all of the flights and hotel rooms whenever we traveled. And while all they wanted to do was either smoke or just do nothing at all, I was spending money to go to Atlanta to push the product I had worked so hard to create. It didn't take long to realize that Keke, Stacey, and I didn't have the same goals in mind. One day while we were having a photo shoot at Keke's house, Stacey felt like it was time to let me know how she truly felt. I was deciding on looks when I noticed that she was sitting back negatively commenting on everything I chose.

"This is all too much, Skittlez," Stacey began.

"What is? We can always choose something else as the first look," I said confused. I was all about Stacey and Keke giving their input. They just never really seemed to care.

"Not the clothes. I mean this whole thing. You went behind our backs. You stole the idea for Cupcake Mafia from us, and now you're the only one getting paid."

During this time, Cupcake Mafia was only a start-up, so I didn't see a dime in profits. I was putting all of my money into it by myself, and I knew that in the beginning, I had to spend money before I made any.

"Stacey, what are you talking about? I'm the only one flying back-and-forth trying to make sure we all eat."

"How? We don't even get a percentage," Stacey said as if she were offended by the fact.

"A percentage? A percentage of what? Ya'll haven't put in any work."

Once I said that, a big argument started. Stacey went on-and-on about how unfair I was, but neither Stacey nor Keke were dedicated to the vision Cupcake Mafia needed to be successful. All they seemed concerned with was making fast, easy money, and receiving free merchandise. After leaving Keke's house, I went to talk to the only person I knew would understand—my godbrother Lo. When I got to his house, I explained what happened, and he wasn't surprised. He had tried to warn me about Keke and Stacey before. But we were really good friends, so I didn't listen.

"They don't have anything going for themselves, and they never will. If you want this thing to be a success, you're gonna have to drop the dead weight."

After that situation, I knew I had to protect myself, so I had Cupcake Mafia trademarked and copyrighted. I wanted to remain cordial with Keke and Stacey, but I knew that we could no longer be friends. I knew that they wanted to see me fail, so my new motivation became to prove them wrong. A couple months after starting Cupcake Mafia, I knew that I needed to get office space. I had been doing all of the shipping and promotion from home, but with Cupcake Mafia picking up, I didn't have the room anymore. And soon, people began to show interest in working for the company as well, but I had nowhere to house them. I had to get an office. After looking at a few spaces, I found the biggest space I could afford. It was about the size of a walk-in closet, but for $500 a month, it was perfect. Once I got settled, I began to put up postings to hire new staff, and I soon hired a few interns and started working on getting Cupcake Mafia's name out there. I worked hard to get my product in wherever I could from fashion shows to different boutiques to different tradeshows even if that meant I had to drive just to get there. I began gifting my t-shirts to different celebrities as a different way of branding. I kept thinking about when D told me, "You are a walking billboard." I knew the same thing would be true for any celebrity who wore my clothes.

    Our small yet effective team consisted of Jennifer who had her degree in marketing; Alicia, who also had her degree in marketing but worked for a business firm; Heather, my assistant; and Clare along with several other interns. We worked in the office together all night after we all got off from our day jobs. We would brainstorm ideas on how to brand ourselves and how to get celebrities into our clothes. By us all wanting to see Cupcake Mafia take off played a huge role in the success of the company. We became like family. Each of my employees came to work wanting to work harder than the day before. We were dedicated. I wanted Cupcake Mafia to be multi-cultural and include every kind of girl. My goal was to create cute, affordable street wear for the girls who feel like they have voice, so I continued to design every single day. I was able to use some of the connections I had made throughout my music career, and the brand started building. We were selling out on the website each week, which was good news, but unfortunately, the printer we were using at the time couldn't keep up with the ever-increasing orders. So we were on the hunt for a new printer. This process took a while because all of the prep work had to be redone and explained. But to quickly remedy the situation, we had to split orders between two printers. As my team grew, I also hired an accountant and a lawyer and contracted other printers in the area to compare prices. Despite all of our hard work, no one was being paid for their efforts, but everyone was willing to sacrifice because we all working for the success of the company. Business was steady, but I knew we needed more, so I hired a web designer who worked in the same building to create a website. At the same time, I had 5,000 fliers printed. We left them everywhere. The team's goal was to pass out at least five fliers wherever we went, and soon Cupcake Mafia received more attention than we ever expected.

"The Cupcake Frenzy in Cleveland," the article read. With the cupcake-scented candles we posted all around the office, and the company's name, word around town was that Cupcake Mafia was a bakery. Despite the obvious error, we were receiving a lot of inquiries, which only gave us more opportunity to reach a larger market and receive new customers through the free promotion. This also gave me an idea that I knew would set us apart from any other clothing company. Even though we weren't actually a bakery that didn't mean we couldn't smell like one, right?

Because we burned cupcake scented candles every day, the clothes inevitably absorbed the smell and soon customers would comment that the product smelled exactly like cupcakes. I knew that packaging was everything. If the package was pretty then the customer would appreciate us going the extra mile of making it smell good too. After researching how to get the vanilla smell into each customer's order, and a lot of trial and error, we found a way to make the clothes smell like cupcakes that was cost effective, but most importantly not time consuming. With the orders growing each day, I had to be smart with our resources. Another aspect of Cupcake Mafia's uniqueness was that we decided to donate a percentage of our yearly profits to the Susan G. Komen Breast Cancer Foundation. After my grandmother passed away from breast cancer, I knew that it was the right thing to do.

In our first year of business, we were a part of the Magic Tradeshow in Las Vegas. I had always been a part of the event as a buyer for Donnard's, but that year, Cupcake Mafia had its own booth. Well, we partnered with another company, but I soon learned that there was little friendly competition in the fashion industry. The company who we shared the booth with thought that we were taking business away from them. The vibe in the room changed, but I tried not to let it bother me.

"Kill them with kindness," I said wanting to reassure my staff, but I needed the reminder as well.

Cupcake Mafia was scheduled to be at the event for two days. The first day was all about my cupcakes, and I intended to take advantage. During our first day, we ended up in fifty stores. And when we got back home, we had to turn a few potential buyers down due to their store policies, but even then, we had more orders than we knew what to do with especially working between two printers. The second day I worked as a buyer for Donnard's. I had been there many times before with Donnard, but for some reason, this time was different. I could tell that he wasn't happy that Cupcake Mafia was invited as well, but I knew that once he saw how it went, he would finally believe in my abilities and me. I mean I wasn't his partner for no reason. But I was wrong. The week before we left, I got a call from the hotel we were staying in stating that the accommodations had been switched. I called Donnard to verify because usually we checked in with each other before making decisions, but he said that he was bringing along a new employee in case I couldn't focus during the show. I tried not to let his doubts affect me, and I let him know that there was no need. I was more than focused. At that time, Cupcake Mafia and Donnard's were my life, and I gave my all to both.

When I met up with Donnard on the second day of the tradeshow, he was attached at the hip with Jaquita, the new buyer he decided to invite at the last minute. He informed me that they would only be doing men's buying that day, so I didn't think twice about it. Honestly, it was my least favorite area, but I later found out that Donnard was training Jaquita to do women's buying right under my nose. I was furious. That was my job, and I was more than capable of doing it, but he didn't see it that way. As the show continued, Jaquita had been buying from all of my established accounts. I had very good relationships with the stores, and they are who informed me of Donnard's newly found buyer, one of them being Jeffrey Campbell. I had been thinking about leaving Donnard's for a while by this time, but just like my relationship with Zahid, I had invested everything I had, and I didn't know if I was ready to let it all go. I tried not to think about it and continued on with the show, but Donnard made it perfectly clear that his attention was solely on Jaquita. Whenever I would find something I liked, I would try to get his opinion on it too. That's how we normally operated, but each time, he would ask, "Why don't you ask Jaquita what she thinks?" The question irked me to no end. Donnard and I were partners. I had taken the sales from just $3,000 a week to over $19,000. Jaquita was new, so I had no problem with her learning the ropes as a buyer. I just didn't want her experience to be at my expense. After a while, Donnard became upset and distant. I fell back and allowed them to lead the way. But not long after, Donnard showed me that my input was no longer needed.

"If you don't really want to be here, you can go back to your own booth."

The words didn't register as they left his mouth until I finally realized that he was talking to me. With tears beginning to well up in my eyes, I grabbed my purse before Donnard got the satisfaction of seeing one fall and headed for the exit. Once I got onto the shuttle, I finally broke down. All of the pain, frustration, and disappointment poured out of me, but right there, I made the decision to leave Donnard's for good. I was willing to figure it out on my own rather than continue to help grow someone else's business. I finally realized that there was no partnership. As long as I continued to work at Donnard's, I would continue to work for him. After I returned home to Cleveland, I officially resigned and placed all of my focus on Cupcake Mafia. There were many times that I just wanted to quit and give up, but I thought about my staff and all they had given up to make my dream a reality. With no room for defeat, Cupcake Mafia continued to grow. And more business meant that we needed more space, so once again my team and I were on the hunt for a bigger office.

Zahid still felt like I put too much time into work. And even after we separated, I was still holding onto what we use to have. I still tried to repair my marriage, but the demand on my time grew as I continued to work between Donnard's and Cupcake Mafia. Honestly, I just didn't have the time. But by the time I left Donnard's, Zahid and I were completely separated and living in separate places because no matter how many times we tried, our relationship remained the same. After I left from the condo we shared, I didn't know if divorce was really the answer. I just needed some space. But as time went on, getting a divorce seemed like the best solution especially after Dre appeared back in my life. While Zahid and I were separated, he became the only person who I could talk to. I wasn't looking for another relationship, but it was nice to speak my mind with no judgment and actually have someone listen. And to my surprise, after everything that I told Dre about Zahid and me, he still encouraged me to stay and work it out. He would always say that he would hate for me to regret not putting my all into Zahid when my heart was still with him, but by that time, I didn't think that it was anymore. And as much as I tried to fight it because I knew that my life was too complicated to involve anyone else in, my feelings resurfaced for Dre. He quickly let me know that he felt the same, but he was uncomfortable dating a married woman. In my heart, I wasn't. I had given Zahid three years of my life, and each year continued to be worse than the last. I knew that he and I were no longer right for each other, but neither of us knew how to let go. But in June 2012, I took the first step to free both of us from the domestic hell we had created for ourselves.

***

It had been three months since Zahid and I spoke when we arrived at the courthouse. He made it a point to remind me that if I went through with the divorce that I wouldn't see a dime, but he had tormented me for years, so I was fine with that. Once the court proceedings were over, Zahid passed me in the hall and said, "Your life will never be the same without me. You should have never done this." Not even five minutes after leaving the court, his torment continued. Despite all, that he had put me through, divorcing Zahid was the last thing I wanted to do. I had helped to create the man he was without asking for anything in return. All I wanted was for him to love me the same way that I had loved him, but like many things in our relationship, his love got lost in translation, and soon I realized that I deserved better. I deserved to be happy, and for the first time, I put myself first.

Later that day, Zahid showed up at my house. I was in no mood for his usual antics, but with tears in his eyes and regret on his face, he had convinced me to hear him out.

"Now that we're divorced, we can start over," he pleaded.

I rolled my eyes at the idea, but the more I thought about it, the more it made sense. Maybe all of the pressure we had in our lives was what drove us apart. I still loved Zahid, and I knew that he loved me too, so I rationalized the idea of us starting over again. I had invested over three years of my life into him, and all I kept hearing was, "Why would you build a plane from the ground up…" I didn't want any other girl taking my place alongside him. I had to fight for what was mine despite the fact that I had fought so hard to let it go. Falling victim to the comfort I felt with Zahid, I agreed to give our relationship one last chance, and that chance lasted only three weeks. During the time that Zahid and I had gotten back together, I realized that the chemistry just wasn't there anymore. I continued to hold onto a relationship that had died long ago in fear of what the future held. I knew I had hurt Dre during my brief reconciliation with Zahid, but that was the last thing that I ever wanted to do. I honestly felt like I was caught in between the two, but after realizing that there was no fixing Zahid and me, I decided to give Dre the chance he deserved.

    To get my mind off my romantic troubles, I threw myself into my work. I started traveling back-and-forth to Atlanta where I began to book more styling jobs as well as continued to promote Cupcake Mafia. While there, I styled Zahira from Omggirlz amongst other celebrities in Atlanta, and I realized that if I wanted to be a household name, I was going to have to leave my hometown of Cleveland for good. Not long after I came back to Ohio, I picked up the business and moved to Georgia. My whole team was upset because they thought that I was throwing away all of the hard work they had put into the company, but once I left, they realized that I was only trying to pave the way for us all. The move was not only a sacrifice for them, but for me as well. I was pretty much back at square one, and I was doing everything out of my house by myself once again. Also with the move, I noticed that my profits decreased. I knew that I would need to get a second job just to supplement my income, but trying to look for a job as a stylist or buyer left little room for Cupcake Mafia. Although it seemed like the right decision, I stepped out on faith and focused all of my energy into the business. And soon I noticed my sales increase again. My faith was restored that I was following the path that God had set out for me.

    Dre and I were still dating, but I noticed that I was complacent in our relationship. We only really saw each other twice a month, but after being in such a controlling relationship with Zahid, it was nice to have a little space. With Cupcake Mafia growing by the day, we began to be showcased on popular television shows such as *Love & Hip Hop* and *T.I. & Tiny*, which helped to grow the brand even more. But in midst of all of our success, I realized that Dre didn't understand my business ethics at all, and soon that caused a strain in our relationship. And even though we had similar pasts, we didn't have similar futures. I was willing to invest my last dollar into Cupcake Mafia, but Dre didn't see the point.

"If you would stop spending so much money...," he would always say.

Soon his negativity became draining, and I felt like I was with Zahid all over again. Not willing to go down the same path I had before, I decided to focus on work rather than Dre and his opinions. I had more than enough experience with men who could never respect my hustle, and honestly, it was getting old. I tried to give Dre the benefit of the doubt though when he surprised me with a trip out of the country for my birthday. I was excited for the much-needed vacation, but once we arrived, Dre started to act weird. I later found out that he was still talking to one of his ex-girlfriends. His deceitful ways ruined my birthday, but I had enough heartbreak to last a lifetime. I was saddened by the situation, but it was the best thing that could have happened to me. Little did I know that soon every piece of my life would fit into place perfectly at just the right time.

***

What is a soul mate? A soul mate is like a best friend but more. It's the one person in the world who knows you better than you know yourself. Someone who inspires you to be a better person. A soul mate is someone you carry with you forever. It's the one person who knew you, and believed in you when no one else would. And no matter what happens, you'll always love them, and nothing could ever change that.

In 2011, I met the man I would fall deeply in love with even though I couldn't see it then. I had been hurt so many times before that I wasn't ready for anything serious. When I met my boyfriend Alphonso, we connected right away. He was a buyer from out of state, and he was the owner of House of Magic Boutique. He was only a year older than I was, but he had already been in business for ten years. We both had the same passion for fashion and travel, and I fell in love with his drive and ambition. We only talked maybe once a month in the beginning, but our conversations seemed endless. Soon he began to carry Cupcake Mafia in his store, so we initially connected on more of a business level. But after running into him at a tradeshow, Alphonso finally made his intentions known.

"When are we gonna link up?" he asked with a smile on his face. We had never flirted with each other before, so the request caught me off guard.

He ended up asking me to dinner that night, and I can happily say that we have been together ever since. We became inseparable. I had been mistaken before, but everything about him felt different. He was truly genuine. He had encountered many hard times growing up just as I had, and he was in the same industry, so he understood what I was going through because he had been there too. He would reassure me that everything was all a part of the process, and I was on the right track. His love for God was what I admired the most. We both were very religious, so he encouraged me to get back into church and seek God. He wasn't perfect, but I knew that he was perfect for me. And after he stole my heart, I didn't see any other man. My past meant nothing anymore, and all of the heartbreak I had endured suddenly hurt less. After finally receiving my happy ending, for the first time in my life, I could just be Mary. But with Alphonso and I both being business owners, time was extremely important to us. We vowed to each other that no matter how busy we were, we would always make time to spend together. And being that we both loved fashion, we have been able to work together as well.

Cupcake Mafia continued to grow more than I could ever imagine. We are now in over 500 stores and 15 countries. We currently ship over 500 orders bi-weekly. We have two showrooms in Cleveland and Atlanta, and we're also collaborating with Jeffrey Campbell on a project, which launches in August 2014. Although I am thankful for the success that we have received so far, this book was to inspire little girls all over the world to follow their own dreams. If I can do it, you can too, but it takes hard work, dedication, and passion to be successful. My story is far from perfect, but I have been blessed with positive people around me from my boyfriend, to my Cupcake Mafia team, to all of my family and supporters, so just know that this is only the beginning. There is so much more in store for us…

Keep Dreaming, Cupcakes,
Mz. Skittlez

TURN THE PAGE TO READ MORE ON HOW TO CREATE A SUCCESSFUL T-SHIRT BRAND THE RIGHT WAY!

AFTER THAT HEAD OVER TO SHOP WWW.CUPCAKEMAFIATS.COM
SPECIAL DISCOUNT PROMOCODE- ICING

The Ingredients to Start an Amazing T-shirt Line:

1. Come up with a marketable idea that's different from what's on the market

After you've decided that you want to start you own t-shirt business, start brainstorming about possible ideas for your t-shirts. Write down as many ideas as you can. Some things to think about are do you want text shirts or graphic shirts or both? Do you want to make shirts for women, men, or babies? Is this idea out already? What is hot right now and what is everyone wearing? Do you want color shirts, or mostly black or white shirts? The more questions you ask yourself, the more ideas you will come up with during your brainstorming session.

Ask yourself:

- Why is your t-shirt brand is more than just about selling t-shirts?
- What your t-shirt brand stands for?
- How can you create a strong visual identity for your brand?
- What void in the market are you filling?

2. Determine your target market

After you've brainstormed your ideas, it's time to start thinking about your target market. Who do you want to sell your t-shirts to? Be as specific as possible. "Women between the ages of 18-45" is not a specific target market. You must dig deeper and find your niche. Some examples of target markets are skateboarders, women who have toddler children, grandmas or grandpas, Las Vegas tourists between the ages of 25-45, men who play golf, etc. The possibilities are endless and the more specific you can get with your niche market, the easier it will be to sell your shirts and come up with specific marketing plans.

3. Set up your business structure

Most t-shirt entrepreneurs start out as a sole proprietor, but as their company and sales grow, they change their company structure to an LLC, LLP, or corporation. Think about how big you want your business to be and then consult with a business or legal professional on what the ideal business structure would be for you. Another thing you might want to consider is what type of sales you want to focus on – retail (selling directly to consumers), wholesale (selling to other stores) or both. This might help you decide what business structure is best for you.

3.5 Don't Just Jump Out there…

Create products people would actually buy. It seems this step should be obvious, but you'd be surprised at some of the t-shirts you can find these days. Test the quality of your t-shirts by getting honest opinions from others, preferably people who are within your target audience.

4. Manufacturing your t-shirts

Many t-shirt entrepreneurs start out by purchasing t-shirt 'blanks' from other manufacturers. This allows them to offer a variety of sizes, colors and styles, but keep costs to a minimum. Many t-shirt blank manufacturers have really low minimums, so you can test a few different styles to see what will sell best for your niche market. Another option is to have a t-shirt manufacturer make shirts according to your specifications, but they often require you to purchase thousands of shirts at a time, which might not be feasible when you first start your shirt business. If you search for "shirt blanks or shirt manufacturers," you will be able to find a plethora of resources online. Get a few samples made and ask your friends and family what they think.

5. *Printing your t-shirts*

Some people get in the t-shirt business because they love to screen-print and they have all the necessary equipment to print their own t-shirts. If that's not you, then search the Internet for screen printers in your local area and meet with them to discuss your needs. Don't be afraid to interview a few screen printers and work with the one who is a good fit for you.

6. *Pricing your t-shirts*

The price of your t-shirts depends on what it costs you to make each t-shirt. When calculating the price, make sure to include the actual price of the shirt, screen-printing costs, shipping costs, costs of hangtags and labels and other costs such as marketing, storage/warehousing and labor. Also, consider if you plan to sell retail, wholesale, or both. If you are not selling your shirts to other stores or boutiques, then you might be able to price them lower since you are cutting out the middleman. Set a price that allows you to cover all the costs and make a profit as well. And don't be afraid to price your shirts higher if your costs justify it.

7. *Storing and shipping your t-shirts*

Many shirt entrepreneurs start out by storing their shirts in their garage, basement, or home office in bins or on shelves. Think about how much time and space you have and what you want to focus your efforts on.

Do you enjoy packing and shipping and do you have the time to do it? If so, starting in your home is a good idea. But if you hate the idea of going to the post office every day or if you don't have space in your house to store your shirts, then consider hiring a fulfillment house, which will do all the storage, packing and shipping for you for a fee.

8. Selling your t-shirts retail

If you want to sell your shirts directly to the consumer, it's probably a good idea to set up your own website and print some postcards so you can promote your t-shirt business. Websites such as Wix, Big Cartel, and Big Cart are great sites to get you started. Allow people to purchase items directly from your website and make sure you have good photography that reflects the quality of your t-shirts. You might also want to consider selling your shirts at local events such as flea markets, fashion shows, or street fairs or fundraising events.

9. Selling your t-shirts wholesale

You can also sell your shirts to other stores that target your niche market. These can include local boutiques, gift stores, t-shirt shops, and even larger retail chain stores. You can call the store directly and ask to speak to the buyer. Many stores like supporting businesses in their area, so it's best to start out with stores in your town or city first. After you got your brand in a few stores, then try trade-shows.

10. Marketing and promoting your t-shirts online and offline

Just because you have a website doesn't mean that swarms of people will know about it or even find it online. It's best to work with your web designer to make your website search engine friendly so people can easily find you. Contact other businesses and ask to exchange links, post comments on other people's blogs (with a link back to your online store) and partner with websites that target your niche market but don't compete with you. Send products to celebrities, local bloggers, and many

Lastly, wear your t-shirts as often as you can! This is often of the best and most effective method to get your shirts seen. Tell everybody you know about your new business venture and ask them to tell their friends. Word of mouth is very powerful. Free advertisement is your best friend. Use so many different outlets

10.5 Come up with a promotion strategy.
Figure out a way to spread the word in a manner that those who discover your brand go on to spread the word to others. For starters, your strategy can include PPC ads, press releases to blogs, and social networking. You can even give away t-shirts with your logo for free. Using guerrilla tactics and promotional items like this can have a tremendous impact on your business growth. However, don't be a Cheapo. Sooner or later, you'll realize that you're going to have to spend money to market your t-shirt business, so you should be willing to pay for things like online ads, event sponsorships, and other paid marketing methods. Understandably, not everyone is rollin' in the dough, so find smart ways to balance paid promotion with free promotion to create an excellent strategy.

11. Set business goals.
How many t-shirts do you plan to sell this year? How about this month

or this week? A lot of people new to the business have no idea, or just don't care. Then there's the group of people who are too scared to set a goal out of fear that they won't reach it. A successful business sets goals of success, in order to have a solid idea of what it's working towards. Set a goal and believe in your ability to reach it. As the law of attraction goes: if you know you're going to reach it, you're going to reach it. If you decide from this day forward that you will sell 10 t-shirts every week, and strongly believe in your business, you'll do everything you can to figure out a way to get those tees moving. If you don't set a goal, well of course, you'll be stuck with a box of t-shirts you were too scared to sell.

12. Don't quit because you're not seeing sales the first day.

That's a good way to get you nowhere. Try to figure out ways of improving your designs, your strategy, or your work habits. When you're just getting started, you're still learning so keep at it. Winners never quit and quitters never win. Read informative, motivational books, to keep your spirits up. Frequently visit other brand's websites and blogs, and see how much fun they're having, to remind yourself of where you want to be in a few years and how bad you really want it. Reanalyze your business plan, promotional efforts, and branding strategy. Consider how you compare to the competition and emphasize your competitive edge.

13. Have fun be SWEET!

If you're in it just to make a quick buck you're not going to succeed– and that goes for ANY business. Love what you do and do what you love. Your passion will definitely show in your brand image. The more fun it is, the more productive you'll be. Just don't get too carried away…on second thought, go ahead every minute counts.

More details and steps to grow your business coming soon:
How to Grow When Times are Slow 101 seminars will be available on mzskittlez.com

Thank you so much for taking the time to purchase my debut novel "The Icing on Top Isn't Always Sweet. This has been a long time coming and my ultimate goal is to inspire those who often think about giving up. Before you close this book, I just need you to do a few things for me, please take out the order form behind this page, and give it to someone else. Also, head over to Amazon and leave your positive review on the book. After that, take a picture of the book and hashtag #Icingontop #Mzskittlez I want to know who you are and personally thank you for your purchase. The time you have taken out to read this book means so much to me. I am looking to unite the world together one cupcake at a time and you can help by following the simple steps above.

Thanks Mary Skittlez Seats
www.mzskittlez.com

Mz. Skittlez

"The Icing on Top Isn't Always Sweet"

This book is for people who thought about giving up, and people that think their ideas are too big to fulfill. People who think they need investors to grow their business from the start. All moguls started with a dollar and a dream.
Never give up or take no for an answer!

It's yours if you want it bad enough....
you can turn every tragedy to triumph.
If this book helped you in any way
please take out this
order form and give it to someone to
help them. Fill out this form below and
send it in for a signed copy for a friend
or family member.
Please leave comments on
Amazon

The Icing On Top Ain't Always Sweet

SEND $15.00 TO

Cupcake Mafia | 650 Hamilton Ave | Suite K | Atlanta, Ga | 30312

ORDER FORM

Please send me _____ copies of "The Icing on Top Isn't Always Sweet" $15.00 plus $8.00 shipping. Enclose a check or money order for $_____ made payable to Cupcake Mafia.

Name:_____

Address:_____

_____

Tel:_____

Email:_____

Mz. Skittlez

Meet the Author

Mary 'Mz. Skittlez' Seats born on May 22, 1987 in Cleveland, Ohio is a celebrity stylist, artist, and CEO of Cupcake Mafia. Ever since Skittlez was young, she always had big dreams and was full of determination. She grew up in community where money was scarce, but fortunately, the lack of resources forced her to creatively use what she had. At the age of 13, she began making clothes, putting various colors in her hair, and laying the groundwork of what would become her signature style. Music has been a part of her life as far back as she can remember. And while attending elementary school, she found her passion in entertainment, but it wasn't until high school that she slowly emerged as a very talented female rapper. B[...] best friends in ninth grade, her life took a tu[...] way to cope, she took a pen and a pad and began writing. Skittlez knew that the only way she would be able to tell her story was through her music. Although her confidence and optimism persevered in her the passion for rap, it wasn't until her senior year of high school that she became serious about her music. Skittlez's fast rise to fame became apparent among her classmates. And with such an a[...]eal, she took the initiative to distinguish h[...]ers in her area. During the summer of 2[...], she went into the studio to record her very first major track, and as a result, her admiration for music fostered many more songs. But in the midst of her success, another tragedy prevailed again in the death of her older sister Denise McCoy. After finding out her sister committed suicide, she realized that her music was her only way out.

In 2007, Skittlez yearned to deliver a message to her listeners that would allow them to relate to her unfortunate experiences while remaining responsible and mature. Although she was very successful, soon music wasn't enough, so she decided to use her styling skills and fashion expertise to start her own clothing line. In 2011, Skittlez launched Cupcake Mafia with only $300 and 30 t-shirts. Its purpose was to ignite an intense movement of uniqueness and originality. With just an office space the size of a closet and a dream, Skittlez and her team worked every day to see the company succeed. And in just three short years, Cupcake Mafia is now located in over 800 stores and 15 countries.

While Skittlez and Cupcake Mafia have been successful, she never misses an opportunity to give back. The Save the Cupcake Foundation is dedicated to the research, cure, and education of Breast Cancer awareness for women. 20% of Cupcake Mafia's proceeds go to the Susan G. Komen Breast Cancer Foundation. Her dedication for the cause is due in part to the loss of her grandmother to breast cancer, and as a result, she has used her love of fashion to keep her grandmother's memory alive.

This future mogul refuses to let anything get in her way!

Made in the USA
Columbia, SC
02 February 2020